SONIC

MY AUTOBIOGWOOFIE

As told by Sonic himself

(With a little help from his P.A/Mum
Diane Bowker)

Published in 2013 by
Diane Bowker

Printed in 2013 by
CPI UK

ISBN: 978-0-9574953-1-9

Revised Edition

© Copyright 2008 held by Diane Bowker
The Author asserts her moral right to be identified as
the author of this work.

All rights reserved. No part of this publication may
be reproduced, stored in a retrieval system, or
transmitted, in any form or by any means, electronic,
mechanical, photocopying, recording or otherwise,
without the prior permission of the copyright owner
and publisher.

CONTENTS

1. Life on the streets
2. My birthday
3. Kennel life
4. The day I chose my Mum and Dad
5. The visits
6. What, No breakfast?!
7. Happiness has its price
8. Going home!
9. Home sweet home
10. A lot to learn
11. Rude awakening
12. Raining carrots
13. Working 9-5 (my first day at work)
14. Weekends are great!
15. The great escape (not so great actually)
16. Meeting the Kent pack
17. Redundant
18. Life on the dole
19. The photo shoot
20. Dew claws…..WHY?!
21. Meeting the seaside pack
22. My first proper Christmas
23. New Year new pals
24. Redundant AGAIN
25. The big bird house
26. Home alone
27. The kitchen demolition
28. Problem solved or double trouble?
29. Internet dating

CONTENTS

- 30 THE ONE
- 31 Our first date
- 32 The long wait
- 33 The day that Speck came home
- 34 Our first night together
- 35 Speck learning the ropes
- 36 Speck's health scare
- 37 Speck meets the Kent pack
- 38 The routines of everyday pack life
- 39 Open day at the vets
- 40 Laminated nightmares
- 41 Speck meets the magical tree
- 42 Our first Christmas together
- 43 My New Year wishes

This book is dedicated to all of you wonderful, kind, caring, very special people that work at Battersea Dogs and Cats home, Castledon Kennels, and all the many other rescue centres worldwide.
You spend your lives working around the clock to rescue, rehabilitate and re-home dogs like Sonic and Speck, and for that we are forever in your debt.

Thank you.

☺ xx ☺

50% of the profits from the sale of this book will be donated to dog rescue charities including Battersea Dogs and Cats home and Castledon Kennels

A WORD FROM DIANE, SONIC'S MUM / P.A

Have you ever looked into a dog's eyes and wondered just what goes on in that furry little head?

Well, after sharing my life and home with many 4-legged friends over the years, I have come to the conclusion that an awful lot goes on in there!

Dogs come in all shapes, sizes and colours. There are clever dogs, not quite so clever dogs, energetic dogs, lazy dogs, happy dogs, grumpy dogs, outgoing dogs, shy and reserved dogs, obedient dogs and naughty dogs. The list is endless; however, one thing that they have in common, is that they are all special and they all deserve the same love and respect from us, their human companions, that they lavish unconditionally upon us.

All of my dogs have been very different in looks and personality. All have been rescue dogs and very special and precious to me, and all of those that are sadly no longer with me, are remembered fondly and missed terribly.

I have often looked into Sonic's eyes and wondered just what goes on in his furry little head.

He looks right back into my eyes and knows precisely what goes on in mine, because despite my best efforts, he is always one step ahead of me.

He spends a lot of time just looking and listening to things that go on around him, and I know that he is working out what his life is all about. I am convinced that he not only figures things out, he also plans things as well.

In fact Sonic is a lot more human than some humans are.

I wish that Sonic could speak, as he really does have so much to say for himself, but despite being an extremely clever lad, being born a dog sadly didn't equip him with the physical capabilities of speech, unlike Jack parrot who is a very vocal member of the family.

As I know Sonic well and have a pretty good idea of what does go on in his furry little head, I have taken the liberty of writing his life story down for him as I know he would like it to be told.

Sonic's life before Battersea is a bit of a mystery, so is based on assumption, but all of the post-Battersea stories are based on events that really happened.

Sonic is a Lurcher and true to his breed, is a bit of a 'Drama Queen' by gene default, so in keeping with his typical fun loving, outgoing Lurcher personality, his stories have been subjected to just a little exaggeration and elaboration in places.

Most of the characters, both canine and human, are real, though some of their names have been changed to protect their privacy.

This book was actually written in 2008 and has spent the last few years sitting in our spare room waiting for me to get my act together and get it published, but due to lack of time and finances it has always been put aside to 'do another day'. Finally that day has come.

Sadly, since this book was written, we have lost some very dear friends. They will all be sadly missed, but never forgotten and will always be in our hearts, and remembered within the pages of this book.

Local rescue kennels and many other lovely people were kind enough to give us their support, and we owe it to them and all of those great dogs still in rescue centres, to finally get Sonic's story told. I can only apologise profusely to all concerned for the very long delay in doing so.

I would like to say a huge thank you to Sonic's Aunty Debs, for kindly sparing her valuable time and expertise to help us with this book.

Life with Sonic and his beautiful girl Speck has certainly been an adventure for us all, and I am happy to say that it still is and I hope will always be, for a very long time yet.

There have been many new adventures over the last 4 years. Speck has blossomed and matured into a sensible young lady, but Sonic it seems, is destined to be the perpetual puppy!

As with us humans, dogs are individual characters with their own little ways and endearing, or not so endearing little quirks.

Also as with us humans, there are occasionally ones that have that little something extra... The canine X-Factor.

Biased I may be, but I believe that Sonic is one such dog.

I will now leave you in Sonic's capable paws!

Over to you Sonic.................................

Hello Dear Reader

This is my Autobiogwoofie, and my very first attempt at dictating a book.
I have heard that it is customary, and also a great opportunity, to say thank you to everyone that has given their help and support, so here goes:-

HEARTFELT WAGS AND SLOBBERS TO:-

The lovely people who rescued me from the streets and kindly took me to Battersea Dogs home.
If you guys are reading this, thank you from the bottom of my big old heart. You saved me.

All of the wonderful staff at Battersea Dogs and Cats Home, who took great care of me during my stay, and fully restored my slightly wavering faith in humans.

Jodie, Sandra and all the staff at Castledon Kennels in Essex, who spent many months of their precious time, patiently and gently coaxing my poor Speck out from her reinforced shell, and for getting her tail to wag again. And of course a huge thank you for letting her come home to live with me.

My extended human family, for always inviting me and Speck to family parties (I especially enjoy the little people's ones, where we can usually steal toys as well as food). Also, for the lovely Christmas presents that we get every year.
Our toy box overfloweth!

My vet and good friend John and his staff, for taking good care of me and Speck, and especially for showing Mum how to deal with my embarrassing little problem. You will just have to use your imagination here, but if you need a clue, it concerns the 'non barking' end! Although I am about to tell you all about my life in great detail, I am not going to elaborate on this. Some things are just too personal and delicate be shared-even with you, lovely Reader. However, if you were to have a pig's ear or two tucked in your pocket, I may just be persuaded to tell all.

Thanks also to the nice vet that treated my upset tummy, and the nice emergency vet that knocked me out (What was that amazing sleep stuff?!) and relieved me of that very painful broken dew claw. I have never had any more trouble with it, and that was the best hours sleep I ever had!

Thanks to Victoria Stilwell 'It's Me or the Dog' for training Mum and Dad (via the TV box) to be better pack members. With her guidance, they do a pretty good job of working out what goes on in our furry little heads, which I have to say, is not always to our advantage, but me and Speck know who's really in charge. I think they do too, though we let them pretend to be pack leaders now and then.

I am proud to say that we are most definitely not 'problem' dogs, but occasionally play up just so that they can practice their leadership skills. It keeps them on their paws and keeps us amused!

Dad very often says that Victoria would always be welcome to train him personally. I think he is being cheeky, as this is usually when Mum whacks him with something.

Anyway, me and Speck think that Victoria is great and love to sit and watch her working her magic on those poor 'problem' pooches and their even more problematic humans. (Mum has photographic and video evidence of me with my eyeballs glued to the screen, afraid to blink in case I miss something.)

Last but not least, thank you to Mum and Dad for loving us to bits and for putting up with me wrecking the fence, demolishing the kitchen (I now realise this was wrong), stealing food at every opportunity, getting mud and hair and worse all over the house (including on and in their bed) and throwing up in the car on practically every trip.

Apologies to poor Dad, who was left abandoned to fend for himself (I know how he felt) whilst me and Mum were barricaded in the spare room writing this, and thanks also for helping us with the 'technical stuff'.

Mum had to translate doggie lingo into human lingo. We have this telepathic link you see. I would have typed it myself, but my paws are just too big for the keyboard and the words come out like this……….
Pljgnjkjifjneuomrelliitrs... Well, that's what I tell her anyway. Oh perleeeeze! I am a Lurcher and must therefore live up to the intelligent, but extremely lazy reputation of my breed. You know what they say…
Why keep a human and type yourself? ☺

ABOUT ME......................

I am a tall, tan and white, muscular, handsome, intelligent and very modest Lurcher with a psychotic tail (I'll elaborate on this a little later).

Some very kind and lovely people rescued me from the streets and I was taken as a stray, to Battersea Dogs Home in London.

I have lived with Mum (Diane) and Dad (Gary) in Berkshire for the last 2 years now and my beautiful Girlfriend Speck, joined our pack a year ago.

Also sharing our home are the birds: 3 rowdy Cockatiels called: Pickle, Lilli and Peregrine, and a very noisy, sneaky, manipulative smart ass Parrot called Jack, who hates me.

I would like to explain and apologise in advance for any bad things that I have said in this book about small dogs.

I will 'fess up' and be totally honest with you here.

I really don't dislike small dogs at all. In fact I love small dogs really. Some of my best friends are a lot smaller than me. I respect all my fellow canines, big or small, but sometimes I can't help getting very envious of small dogs, because they are so cute and appealing, and I am not.

If you had spent weeks behind bars watching so many lovely people quickly passing you by to rush over and coo over a tiny, fluffy scrap with huge eyes in the kennel opposite, right under your very nose, you might feel the same. So, if I am ranting on about small dogs, please remember that I really, really don't mean it…. Much!

There is much speculation amongst my human pack members, regarding my pre-Battersea life. My friends at the Kennels think that as I am a large, strong chap I was probably trained as a 'working dog', to hunt rabbits and hares.

It is true that I love to chase small, furry creatures like rabbits and cats (hence the broken fence mentioned earlier), but the truth of the matter is, that I simply want to play with them, not kill them.

Mum has very embarrassing photographic evidence showing me lying down in the garden next to our neighbour's cat as proof of this, as you will see later.

I don't say a lot (I'm the strong, silent type) but I do listen and learn. I learnt all about game strategies from listening to Dad talking to Mum about his

beloved X-Box thingy. I think she finds it all very relaxing as she usually falls asleep. I must admit, my eyelids get heavy after the first 5 minutes, but if you want to learn and get on in life, you have to pay attention, so I applied the imaginary matchsticks, got comfy on the sofa (flat on back with legs in air) and soaked up the information.

It paid off, as I have now created my own personal game strategy, steps A-D as follows:-

A/ I stumble across a small furry potential plaything and it just sits still so I ask it to play (bark in its face).

B/ If it ignores my invitation, once I am absolutely sure that it would rather go deaf than play with me, I graciously retreat (go off in a sulk).

C/ If, joy of all joys, my prayers are answered and it decides to play and it runs, I agree to join in the fun (gleefully chase it).

D/ If it stops and hisses, growls or screams at me, I respectfully cease to bother it any further (turn tail and leg it as fast as I can in the opposite direction!).

Now, even if I do say so myself, I am very swift on the old paws and would have no trouble outpacing a rabbit. I could do it in my sleep, In fact I often do, much to the amusement of Mum and Dad so Speck tells me.

She says that they often laugh at my paws going twenty to the dozen, and my ears and eyes twitching in excitement and concentration. Apparently, they say that I look like a professional gurner throwing some sort of fit. Charming isn't it? You think that you have them fully trained to idolise you and respect you, and that they are well and truly 'under the paw'; but as soon as you are incapacitated and unable to defend yourself, they are laughing at you behind your back.

Anyway, let me explain my own view on hunting.

Let's just say that I was chasing a rabbit and I had it cornered; if it screamed in my ear-as they do, I would run for my life. After all, I would only be trying to play with it.

So, there you have it. My human pack have therefore assumed that because of my playfulness and obvious lack of killer instincts, I was of no use to my former human pack, and was simply discarded and left to fend for myself.

Of course I know what really happened, but I have decided that it is something that I would like to keep to myself and there are two reasons for this…..

1. I had a lot of very bad experiences during this time in my life so would rather just forget it, and never have to 'go there' again.

2. I think it is rather debonair, exciting and appealing to have an air of mystery about oneself, don't you? The ladies certainly seem to love it!

Anyway, the sad fact is that I was dumped like an old piece of unwanted furniture, and had to quickly learn to be brave and take care of myself.

This is my Autobiogwoofie. The true(ish) story of my journey from unloved and abandoned street hound, to pampered couch potato…………..

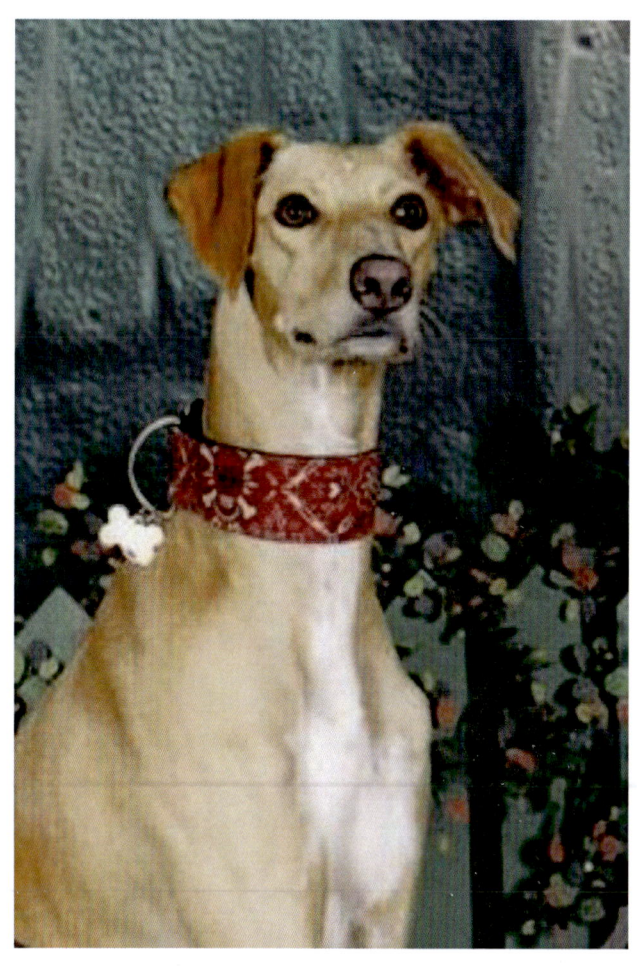

SONIC

Taken at 'The Photo Shoot'
By kind permission of
The Dog Portrait Company

Skinny me soon after leaving Battersea

Chillin in the garden with 'Moo' and 'Boris'

Chapter 1

LIFE ON THE STREETS

It was still winter and very cold. As you may already know, like Greyhounds, us Lurchers also suffer from severe cold and rain allergies. Nowadays, nothing on earth would shift me from my 'forever sofa' out into the rain, but back then I had no other choice. There was no central heating and no 'forever sofa' (2 of my most favourite 'material' things in the world).

At night and on really cold days, I would make a temporary bed under trees by circling round and round in the leaves like my ancestors apparently used to do, and then I would curl up into a really tight ball to try to keep warm.

As I have already explained, I cannot be doing with killing rabbits, so I had to sniff out as many slime-filled snails and slugs as I could find for my dinner. They are not the best tasting meal I have eaten, but when you are starving they taste just fine, and you don't have to use up precious energy trying to catch them. I even sort of liked the crunchy texture, but wasn't so keen on all the slime. Gets everywhere it does, up your nose, between your teeth, and all over your paws and ears. Once I got some in my eyes and couldn't see where I was going and ended up head-butting a lamp post. It was quite painful, but also very lucky, because I needed to lift my leg anyway, and there's nothing quite like a lamp post to announce your presence and ownership of territory to the other lads, and of course the ladies in the vicinity.

There was this one time when I bit into a particularly large snail's shell, it was really tough and made this sort of popping noise, and all this………Oh sorry, are you feeling ill? Ok then, I will move swiftly on.

Each cold, miserable and lonely day just merged into the next, and I was getting extremely thin and had developed sore, itchy skin and itchy, mucky eyes (probably the snail slime).

Although I tried to make myself look and feel all macho and brave, and tell myself that I was doing just fine, deep down I was just a little pup again, lost and alone and scared half to death. Between you and me, I was scared of pretty much everything really. Traffic, sudden noises in the night, the dark, rabbits etc.

I just wanted to be loved and taken care of by a family of my own. Despite all that had happened to me, I did, still do, and always will love humans very much and will greet complete strangers in the street as enthusiastically as if I have known them all my life. Sometimes, I successfully manage to pin them down, and they frantically struggle to get away, but I just cannot bear to let them go without a big old slobbery kiss to take home with them. I always try my best to plant a muddy paw print on their forehead and lovingly rub some of my hair off onto their clothes to remember me by, but they usually manage to wriggle free and get away before I can complete the whole process.

I know that some poor dogs, like my dear Speck (you will get to know her a little later on), who have been through bad times, are quite wary for a very long time, and are even terrified of people, but not me. Soppy old Sonic still loves everyone.

Chapter 2

MY BIRTHDAY

One day, whilst foraging for my usual dinner of…ok, ok, I won't mention snails again, I was having one of my daydreams of pinning down a 'little person' and smothering them with slobbers (I especially love little people – kids you call them) when I spotted some extra friendly looking humans in the distance. They looked over at me, and I felt the old tail starting to twitch.

Ok, let me just pause here to tell you about my psychotic tail - see, I promised I would elaborate.

It has a mind of its own this thing. It might be stuck to my butt, but I have no control over it whatsoever. When I feel excited or happy, it does its own thing. It begins as an involuntary twitch, then quickly steps up to a gentle sway, then progresses to a moderate side to side thrashing motion. The next stage is quite embarrassing. The thing cranks up and starts to go round at high speed in complete 360 degree circles, and sometimes even changes direction, almost knocking me, and anyone in the vicinity, off balance.

I swear to God that some days I have to dig my toenails into the ground to stop myself from taking off! Nowadays when it happens, Mum says that I've got 'the windmillbutt' again. There is also a sort of 'knock on effect' stage to it which often occurs when I am totally beside myself with excitement.

There is so much power and energy thundering up and down the length of my tail, that it has a ripple effect along my body, right up to the tip of my nose giving me the appearance of a big old brown wriggly, hairy snake.

To make matters even worse, the tip of this rebellious, uncontrollable abomination of nature is brilliant white, and sports extra-long, wispy hairs, which for some reason known only to herself, Mum has nicknamed my twizzle.

The twizzle comes in two different seasonal forms, the summer twizzle, and the winter twizzle.

The summer version is slightly shorter and more manageable, and the winter one is longer and more feathery.

I also have summer and winter knickers to match it. In the summer the back of my legs have a slight overlap of fur, that resembles a wispy, tufty seam, but in the winter I get long, feathery wisps of fur in a big ridge all along the backs of my legs. I hold the Saluki gene responsible for this. Thanks a bunch Dad! (my biological Dad that is).

Under normal circumstances, the twizzle is relatively inoffensive, but if it becomes wet, especially the longer winter version after a bath, it dries into this spectacular, firework-like starburst of brilliant white fluff, which is the cause of great embarrassment to me, but causes great hilarity amongst my human pack members.

I even caught Mum sneakily taking a close up photo of it once.

I had already endured the awful indignity of being unceremoniously dumped in the bath earlier on, and then she did that! She actually emailed it to everyone. I was mortified!

Ok, let's get back to the story shall we?.....

My tail was rapidly nearing the windmillbutt stage, so I decided to quickly run over to say hello before it got even worse. However, once I got over there, it was so lovely to have some much needed affection after all this time, that all concerned were subjected to the full Monty (windmill butt and the snake all at once). They didn't seem to mind though and they made a really big fuss of me. I did my best to return the compliment with as much fur sharing, pinning down and slobbering as the poor people could handle.

They were really special people who realised that despite my bravado, I desperately needed help.

Covered in muddy paw prints, hair and doggy drool (yay, the full set!) they took me to a place called Battersea Dogs home in London and for that I will always be eternally grateful to them.

I was handed over to a lady in a blue fleece jumper, who explained that I needed to be checked over. I was told that I had a skin infection, conjunctivitis, a rotten tooth (tell me about it!) and that I was very underweight. Obviously there's not much fat on those old molluscs. See, I didn't say snails did I. Oh, and of course I was host and home to the usual quota of very annoying fleas, tummy worms and just about every rotten little parasite known to dogkind, as is often the case with any respectable stray hound with any street cred.

I was prodded and poked and had a needle in my neck called a vaccination – OUCH! I was given some medicine to deal with my unwelcome lodgers and was then taken to my own little room, complete with a cosy bed, water bowl and toys! And it got even better later on, as I was presented with a bowl of real, proper food, all for little old me. Not a mollusc in sight! I thought I must have died and gone to heaven or was having a lovely dream and would wake up any minute, chewing on one of those you know whats.

I was in what they called the isolation block, and some of my fellow canine kennel guests were finding it all very strange and were having barking matches with each other. I can tell you that despite the racket, I had the best night's sleep for as long as I could remember.

I had a blanket instead of leaves and I was dry and warm with a decent meal digesting in my tummy, and there were no longer any of those nasty little tummy worms to steal it from me while I slept.

As I drifted off into a contented, peaceful sleep, I wanted to remember this day as being my birthday because really, it was. I had been re-born into a better life. It was the 26th March 2006. It was the day that I was saved.

It was My Birthday.

Chapter 3

KENNEL LIFE

After several days, during which I was given these big pink pills which were called anti-biwhatsits or something, for my itchy infections, and these horrible drops in my eyes, (this I did object to!) I was moved into a different block and a little note was pinned to my door, telling prospective new families all about me.

The ladies in the blue fleece had decided to call me Toby. My note said that I was good with children, good with other dogs, and not considered a 'problem' dog. Ha ha! Little did they know! Do they do Dog Oscars?!!

It said on my ticket that I could live in a town or in the countryside and that I may, or may not, have destructive tendencies, whatever that meant? Maybe it meant that I may, or may not eat furniture, kitchens, doors, skirting boards and walls? Well, whatever it meant, I was now considered to be ready to be put up for re-homing at last.

Being an intelligent sort of chap, It didn't take me long to work out the daily routines at the kennels. I was always up early, bright eyed and bushy tailed, full of hope and anticipation at the possibility of being chosen by a family and taken home to be loved, fussed, given access to central heating, beds, toys, sofas and all those other wonderful things that I had heard about, and was longing to try out for myself.

If at the end of the day, you were not lucky enough to be the chosen one, you could console yourself with the thought that dinner would be along soon, and tomorrow was another day, another chance of being chosen, and another dinner!

One of my favourite times of the day was of course meal times. Judging by the deafening explosion of excited barks and howls as soon as the faintest rattle of the food trolley was detected, I was not alone there.

It became a competition amongst us, to try and be the first one to raise the trolley alarm. Every day around meal times, I used to really concentrate and strain my ears to try and pinpoint that first rattle of the wheels of the 'Silver Dream Machine', so called due to it being the sole object of many of my loveliest dreams since arriving at the kennels. I would often wake up dribbling after vividly realistic dreams, where I was being served with choice cuts of tender beef from the sacred silver shelf. On waking, I would always feel a bit embarrassed thinking that I might have been slobbering and chomping my teeth together loud enough for my neighbours next door to hear. Or, God forbid, even worse... whimpering and whining!

Despite my best efforts, I was never able to feel that sense of victory and pride at being the first to raise the food frenzy alarm. I was always out-radared by my kennel mates with the sharpest, most sticky up ears.

Even the Bloodhound types were in with a sporting chance, as though their ears were long and dangly, and consequently even more muffled than mine, their highly honed nostrils could pick up the scent of a single, solitary biscuit crumb a mile away, under water.

I had to face facts. I was a total failure in the trolley detection competition, but, I consoled myself with the thought that if there was ever a race in the kennels with a first prize of a joint of roast beef, I would burn pads and leave those radar-eared suckers standing.

I'd be licking my lips, belching, and contemplating filling up a poo bag at the finish line before they even got their paws over the starting line.

I regularly had visions of that smug little Chihuahua cross in no.18, who had won the trolley competition almost every day since I had been there, left standing there wondering what that brown flash was that whizzed past him. Then upon realising it was me, normally the loser, he starts to yap and spin round in sheer anger and frustration at being defeated by a lanky dog with half-cocked lugs. Then he would head back to his room to sulk.

I could really imagine him doing that. Yes folks, it's a terrible thing to say about a fellow canine, but there you have it. It's just the same as with humans; some dogs are simply just sulky, bad losers. I'm so glad I'm not like that!

Another activity I really enjoyed was walkies time. I would watch with anticipation, for that blue fleece jumper, containing the lovely kennel girl who would take me outside for a nice walk and a gallop around the exercise pen (the girls often changed, but that blue fleece jumper was always the same). Being a typical Lurcher, I have a severe rain allergy and dread going outdoors on wet days. If it was also windy and cold, the girls had more chance of winning the lotto than getting me out there.

I spent 4 weeks at the London kennels and despite my very best efforts, including the odd windmill butt, a snake or two, looking appealing and even trying to make myself look small and cute, instead of tall and gangly, I always heard those dreaded words "I'm really looking for a cute, small one".

I had failed to charm my way into the hearts and homes of any of the people that had visited the kennels in search of a new furry companion.

I couldn't understand why nobody wanted me. Yes I was tall and gangly with short hair, and not small, cute and fluffy, but I was extremely friendly, rather good looking, and stuffed so full of love to give, I was almost bursting at the seams; yet all the lovely people walked on by and chose someone else to take home and love.

Don't get me wrong, I didn't begrudge any of my kennels mates being chosen. Even the little, very cute ones! As I said earlier, I love small dogs really, and every dog deserves the chance of happiness. I was happy for each and every one of them, going off to start their exciting new lives, but I just wished that it was ME!

Eventually, it was decided that I would be moved to try my luck elsewhere, so I was to be transferred to a place called Old Windsor.

I was very excited, as I had overheard kennel gossip that the supreme human pack leader of the whole of England lived nearby in her massive, deluxe Royal Windsor Castle kennel. I had also heard that she liked us canines. I was soon fantasising about being chosen by the pack leader herself, and taken home to live in her Royal kennel (you get a lot of time to daydream in kennels). I would be hand fed with beef, roasted venison and peasant, er I mean pheasant, and have my own kennel maid to throw and fetch sticks for me, and see to it that my every whim is taken care of. And then my exquisite fantasies were suddenly in tatters as I overheard that she only likes Corgis! What kind of Alpha female was this?

Did she not realise how incredibly handsome and debonair us Lurchers are and that we are natural born Monarchy material?! Grrrrr......the world is most definitely ruled by the mini mutts!

Why, oh why was I born with these long, gangly giraffe legs? Why couldn't I have been born small, cute and fluffy, with big sticky up radar ears and stumpy legs? Ah well, never mind, at least I would be able to say that I had Royal neighbours I suppose.

Now, I will be honest here, and admit that I am not the best traveller, and feel queasy at the mere sight of a car or van, so when the time came to drive me to my new kennels, I was more than a little nervous.

By the time I arrived, as well as feeling very sad at leaving my newly acquired friends back in London, I was feeling very scared, and very, very sick.

My normally tan coloured face fur had taken on a definite greenish hue, and my muzzle and front paws were liberally coated with my partially digested, bright yellow breakfast, complete with carrots. How does that always happen? I only had cereal!

What a tragic, terrible waste of my breakfast and what a memorable first impression I must have made on my new carers when they opened up the back of the van.

As in London, my new carers were very kind and patient, and didn't seem to take offence at the messy, smelly consequences of my delicate tummy problem at all. They soon had me cleaned up and checked into my new room. I was hoping for a room with views overlooking the big Royal Castle kennel, but it was much like my old one back in London. I felt a little pang of disappointment, but then immediately felt ungrateful, and deeply ashamed of myself. How dare I have such delusions of grandeur, when I was just a homeless street hound, who a few weeks ago, was laying on wet leaves, cold, alone, scared and hungry. Yup, room number 17 would do me just fine!

Between you and me though, I will fess up to having a dream one night, of me as Royal pack leader to those stumpy, short-legged Corgis. I had those little furballs running to and fro, fetching my toys and sticks. I felt so much better when I woke up!

You must think I am a very sad, bad dog, but you know I really don't mean it, and I really can't control the old green-eyed monster, or what goes on in my overactive imagination while I'm asleep can I?

As the routines at Old Windsor were very similar to those in London, I soon started to feel much better. They also had toys, and that wonderful blue fleece jumper was walking around too! As I mentioned before, it was often a different girl in it, but always a really lovely one. It was a magic jumper indeed!

Best of all though, they also had a sacred Silver Dream Machine! I decided that I rather liked it at Old Windsor.

I wondered if there was a trolley detection competition running in all rescue kennels, maybe even all over the world! There was definitely one running at this kennels too.

I was filled with new hope that as the smug little radar-eared Chihuahua cross was still in London, I might well be in with a shout to win here.

If you are privileged enough to be owned by a canine, you will already know that we are excellent at time management. At the risk of offending you, and I am very sorry if I do, but I have to say we are much better at it than you humans are.

We do not need a ticking time machine to tell us when it is time for dinner, or walkies, or when our family are returning home.

We are all born with an internal clock, tucked safely away in our heads, which never needs winding up, or new batteries and is just as accurate as the clocks and watches that people have to look at when they want to know precisely what time it is.

After my first day of taking in my new surroundings, I was dog tired (pardon the pun) and slept soundly, but I made sure that I was up early the next morning, ready and waiting 5 minutes before the Silver Dream Machine was due to arrive. I was going to win if it was the last thing I did.

I was pressed up against the bars of my room, ears as upright as I could get them (a little more than 45 degrees, which was very good for me), and strained to their absolute limit, tail twitching in nervous anticipation. The minutes ticked by in my head and not one bark or whimper was to be heard. I began to wonder if maybe my fellow residents were still asleep, or maybe they all had Spaniel ears, or maybe there were no Bloodhound types, or no big sticky up ear types, or maybe I was just going to win paws down, fair and square at long last.

I was just trying to decide if I had actually detected the faintest of rattles of the wheels in the distance, or if it had been one of my neighbours stirring next door, when AAAGGHHHHHHH!!!!!! I just couldn't believe it! Frenzied yapping! It had to be a litter-mate of that smarty pants Mexican cross mutt. Or possibly even smarty pants himself! Maybe he had been moved down here too.

I sloped off to my blanket to sulk and try to console myself that I had almost won today and tomorrow
was another day, but the biggest consolation of all was that as always, breakfast was on its way.

Chapter 4

THE DAY I CHOSE MY MUM AND DAD

It was the 3rd of May and a morning much the same as any other. I was dozing peacefully, awaiting the S.D.M to arrive with my breakfast. I had given up wasting my valuable time and energy trying to win the trolley competition.

I had accepted defeat graciously and re-channelled my time and energy into practising my 'smiling' and sad, doe-eyed look in preparation for the days surge of potential new families.

Looking at my irresistible self in the reflection of the bars, I would say that I had it nailed. I actually wanted to adopt myself!

I was determined that I was going to melt hearts. I just felt lucky that day, and instinctively knew that it would be the day that I met my new family. I just had a feeling in my water. Or maybe I just needed to find a lamp post pdq!

It was mid-afternoon and I was getting face ache from constant smiling, eyelash fluttering and trying to make my eyeballs as huge, round and soulful as physically possible. I was exhausted. I had managed to rouse a few mild flickers of interest from some of the people as they passed by, but then those dreaded words would come spilling out…..

"He's friendly, but he's a bit too big" or "I prefer that small one with the sticky up ears" or " he's quite a nice dog, but he doesn't look very cuddly" or "Oh he looks like he needs a lot of exercise" or "can't have that one with the cat, or the kids". These statements were just so hurtful and so NOT TRUE!

Ok, as the subject has come up, let me just deviate for a minute to explain a few things to you about us Sighthounds and hopefully dispel all those awful, incorrect and unjustified things that a lot of people mistakenly think about us:-

Assumption/myth: We look athletic and must therefore feel the need to charge around a field at breakneck speed all day, every day, in hot pursuit of anything that moves.

Truth: We look athletic and feel the need to charge around a field at breakneck speed for approximately 2 minutes in hot pursuit of anything that moves. We then feel the need to spend the next 23 hours, 58 minutes recuperating and relaxing on a comfy sofa, or preferably a human bed.

Assumption/myth: In addition to charging around a field at breakneck speed all day, every day, in hot pursuit of anything that moves, we need to be walked for at least 2 hours twice a day.

Truth: We are extremely lazy, laid back dogs. If we were subjected to this level of exercise, we would quite possibly be deceased within a week. We are graceful, speedy animals, with near zero stamina. Most of us are happy to sleep and laze around for a good 23 hours a day, just getting up for wees, walkies and meals of course.

We are the Cheetahs of the canine world.

Two 20-30 minute walks a day, and a couple of charging around a field at breakneck speed for 2 minutes in hot pursuit of anything that moves sessions once or twice a week, will keep us happy and healthy hounds; anything much more excessive and we will be most put out and unimpressed, and could possibly be filing a cruelty case against you with the R.S.P.C.A!

Assumption/myth: We will chase down and kill any small, furry creatures that are in our sights.

Truth: A few of us given the opportunity, will chase down and kill any small, furry creatures that are in our sights. Hounds that are that way inclined must be muzzled whilst out walking, for the protection of themselves, and all creatures in the vicinity, until they learn that this behaviour is not socially acceptable.

The same can actually be said for any breed of dog. Some are hunters, some are not, it's just that Sighthounds have the speed and agility required to catch almost anything that they decide to chase down and kill.

Some of us (like myself, as you already know), love to chase down any small, furry creatures that are in our sights, but have no intention of killing them. We just want to play with them.

Some hounds have no interest at all in chasing down any small, furry creatures for any reason whatsoever. Many Greyhounds are discarded from racing kennels, because they simply want to play, or they have no natural chase instinct. Not all are discarded for being too slow to race.

Assumption/myth: We cannot live in harmony with other smaller pets, especially cats.

Truth: The vast majority of Sighthounds can be de-sensitised and trained to live peacefully with other pets, even hounds that have been used for hunting or racing. It must be done gradually and carefully of course, with professional advice, especially with those that have chased small, furry things during their career.

As mentioned above, some have no interest in chasing, and will be no problem at all. Some of us (like me) are actually quite afraid of cats!

Assumption/myth: Taking on an ex-racing or hunting dog that has never been in a family home, will be a disaster, as they will have no idea how to behave in a house. The house will be awash with wee!

Truth: Taking on an ex-racing or hunting dog that has never set paw inside a family home, will be an exciting challenge for you, as they will have no idea how to behave in a house.

We Sighthounds are naturally polite and respectful and will be eager to please you, we just need you to teach us your own kennel rules. We learn fast and will be forever grateful to you for giving us a chance to prove that we are wonderful, affectionate, loyal and intelligent dogs. Yes, you might get the odd wet patch on the floor for a few days until we learn that wees are to be performed in the garden only (don't forget we have never had a special wee place before), but once the penny drops (pardon the pun), we will respectfully do our biz outside every time thereafter.

Assumption/myth: I can't have an ex racing/hunting dog as I have children.

Truth: We are bred to be docile, submissive and loyal to all human pack members, big and small, whatever their pack rank. I suppose as with all breeds, there may be a rare exception where an individual does not like children, but most of us like the little people very much. I personally LURVE little people, and will play 'chase me' with them every chance I get! It is very rare indeed for a Sighthound to bite anyone.

We are gentle, sensitive, passive and affectionate souls. I will admit that we can occasionally knock very little people over when we are in mid chase of something, but this would simply be the result of a genuine, clumsy accident, not a deliberate attempt to trample over the said little person. The solution is to prevent such collisions by keeping very little people out of the way when we are running in the garden until they are big enough to join in and play chase with us.

Summary: Sighthounds are true 'people dogs'. We are loyal, affectionate, obedient, intelligent and elegant. We love to be near you. We are lazy. We have severe 'rain and cold allergies' we love to please you. We are clever and fast learners, and dispel that other old myth of 'you can't teach an old dog new tricks'.

Even very old Sighthounds who have spent their entire lives in kennels can be taught to pee only in the garden within a few days.

Sighthounds are also great companions for elderly people as we don't 'get under feet' or need long walks and are happy to just chill out and snore the day away.

Anyway, where was I? Oh yes, 3rd May………

It was mid-afternoon and I was beginning to feel that familiar feeling of failure, when I hear a noise from down the corridor. It was a strange sound that I hadn't heard here before.

I strained my ears to listen and in amongst these weird sounds, I heard people talking.

It was a man and a woman. The voices and strange noises were getting closer.

I heard the man reading out loud what was on everyone's notes on the kennel doors. I was waiting for the usual comments about wanting to take home a mini mutt, but what I heard next was music to my old non-sticky up ears. The man said, (and I quote word for word, as I will never forget it.) "If we are going to get a dog and I have to walk it, we are going to have a proper big dog, not one of these little yappy ones".

I almost fainted with sheer hope and anticipation. This really could be my day; I was defo in with a chance here. I was pressed up against the bars trying to get a glimpse of my potential new pack, but they were not near enough yet. I was praying that they wouldn't take a shine to anyone else before they reached me.

The weird noise was getting louder and I realised that it was coming from the woman. It sounded like an upset sort of noise, um, er…sobbing, that's it. I guess that the rows of pleading eyeballs and sad faces had all got a bit too much for her.

I could hear them talking and making a fuss of my kennel mates as they came nearer and my heart was thudding hard against my skinny ribs as I waited for them to say, "This is the one!" It didn't help my chances to be right at the end of the kennel block, as most people had fallen in love with someone else long before they even got to me.

As they got nearer and nearer I thought I was going to burst with anticipation. My human lingo was not brilliant in those days, but I understood enough to know that they were reading the notes on the doors and were looking for a furry companion that was good with little people.

They apparently had little people in the family that they visited regularly and it was essential to find a dog that wouldn't hurt them. By this time, I was almost peeing myself with excitement. The tail had started its thing, and was well on its way to windmill butt stage when finally, there they were, standing right in front of me.

This was my big chance to shine, my long awaited moment in the spotlight. I just couldn't mess this up.

The man said "I like this one, now that's what you call a real dog!" He said "hello boy" then started to read my notes and apparently, I ticked all the boxes.

The woman crouched down and spoke softly to me.

I desperately wanted her to rub my ears, so I pressed myself hard against the bars, closed my eyes, listened to her voice and imagined the best ear rub a dog could ever have. It felt so real and so soothing that I started to relax and to my great embarrassment, my tail, already in full w.b. mode, suddenly changed from anti-clock to clockwise, then immediately went into snake mode, knocking me off balance and I sort of slithered down the bars into a crumpled heap on the floor.

With my face still all scrumpled up against the bars, I slowly peeled opened my eyes and looked up until they met those of my potential new Mum.

I thought I had blown it, but to my great surprise and relief, it had the opposite effect. She started to sob a bit louder and said that I must be choosing them too. My potential new Dad smiled and said "would you like to come home to live with us boy?"

You bet your life I would!

I tried to get to my feet, to jump up and down with elation, but there was a fanfare blasting in my head and I felt a bit dizzy and my legs buckled up again, so I decided I had better just sit on my tail instead as it was going wild by this time.

I was still reeling from the shock and elation of having finally bagged myself a Mum and Dad at long last, when the fanfare was suddenly cut short by my new Mum saying that she thought it would be a good idea to go round a second time just to make absolutely sure. On hearing this, I immediately went into panic mode. I thought that they would surely change their minds and pick someone else after all.

They said "see you in a minute boy" and walked away. My heart sank and I was thrown into the pit of despair. I resigned myself to thinking that was going to be the last I saw of them. I waited anxiously, face pressed up against the bars for them to come back for me. After a few hours (actually it was only really about 10 minutes, but it felt a lot longer), to my great relief and joy, they re-appeared with smiley faces and told me I was definitely going to be going home with them. I learnt at a later date, that they had actually gone to the kennels looking for a small to medium sized girl, not a giraffe sized boy, so I suppose it was sensible that they made absolutely sure I really was the right boy to join their pack.

They stayed a few more minutes and made a big fuss of me, then explained that they wanted to hurry off to reception to 'reserve me' before someone else got there first. They said that they would come back for me and take me home as soon as possible. And then they were gone.

My new Mum (I liked the sound of that!) started with the sobbing noises again as they walked away.

I had cracked it! Me who never won anything, I was the winner, top dog of the day, a loser no more!

I spent the next hour, pacing around in anticipation for them to come and get me, but they didn't. I was devastated and couldn't understand why they didn't come back.

They had promised they would come back for me and take me home. What was going on? Had they changed their minds?

Just as I was getting into the really dark and gloomy place in my head that I don't like to go to, the blue fleece jumper appeared, containing one of my lovely friends. She said that I was a clever boy and that I had been reserved! I had a new Mum and Dad and a new home to go to. She even wrote 'RESERVED' on my notes in big red letters and gave me a big fuss. Of course I was over the moon. It was really going to happen for me. They did still want me. But where were they? Why was I still here?

My friend explained that there were a few things that had to be done before I was allowed to go to my new home and that I had to be patient. She also said that my new Mum and Dad would visit me and take me for walks around the grounds until I was allowed home. This reassured me a lot, but I was very puzzled. Exactly what were these 'things' that had to be done?

Whatever these 'things' that had to be done were, it would be worth it. I had a home and a family of my own to go to at last. I felt like I had just won the doggie lottery (a lifetime supply of pig's ears).

Chapter 5

THE VISITS

I was still floating on air the next day. The sofa, central heating and all the other super things that I had heard such wonderful stories about would no longer be just objects of my overactive imagination and fantasies. I would soon get to see what they actually looked and more importantly, felt like and they would be all mine to sample and cherish forever!

I would be loved and adored and be a respected member of my new pack. I would have my own bed; (though I would quickly need to establish my rights to the sofa and Mum and Dad's bed too of course), my own toys, my own garden and I would never go hungry again. There would be lovely walks and new friends to play with. Oh, I just couldn't wait!

As they had promised, my new Mum and Dad came to visit me 2 days later and Dad's sister came with them to meet me. She was my new Aunty Louise and she was nice. She said I was a very handsome lad.

I took them for a walk around the grounds. It was wonderful. I felt very special. They sat on the bench and made a fuss of me for ages and we had a run around the paddock too. They were a bit slow and I had to slow down and let them catch me, but I thoroughly enjoyed my game of chase all the same.

Mum sat me down and told me that I would have to have a new name. She said she was sorry if I was going to get confused or upset about it, but she just couldn't cope with calling me Toby. She explained that this was because she knew a great little dog called Toby for many years, but he had sadly passed away. The lady that Toby lived with was very dear to Mum too and she had also sadly passed away.

So I, Toby, was re-christened Sonic. I didn't mind at all really, because I hadn't had much time to get used to my Toby name anyway and Sonic was a cool name.

Right, now this is the perfect time to explain once and for all, the true meaning of my name to avoid any further painful and distressing misunderstandings....

My new name was chosen carefully to compliment my character. It does, of course, represent awe-inspiring, super-sonic speed, power, grace and beautiful, sleek, dynamic looks that are ME to a tee.

It has absolutely nothing to do with fast moving cartoon characters of any kind, so please just do not go there, ok!

I just wish that I had a pig's ear for every time some smarty pants says: "but why is he called Sonic when he's smooth-coated and brown and not spiky and blue?" Grrrrrrrrrrrrrrr......Grrrrrrrrrrr.

Anyway, where was I? Oh yes, I had a lovely time with Mum, Dad and Aunty Louise, then to my great confusion and disappointment, they took me back to the blue fleece, gave me a cuddle and said they would see me in a few days for another visit. Mum went all blurry eyed again and they walked off without me. I just didn't understand why they weren't taking me home with them. Most of my kennel mates went home with their new families either the same day or a couple of days after being chosen. What was going on?

Mum and Dad came to see me again 2 days later and we had another lovely time out walking. I prayed that this time, I would at last be going home with them, but after about an hour, they took me back to the blue fleece lady. Once again, they gave me a hug and said goodbye and that they would see me soon. I was totally flummoxed by this. I wanted someone to explain why I was not in their car and on my way to my new life. There was a sofa and a bed with my new name on them waiting there for me for goodness sake!

Just as I was settling myself into a sulk for the rest of the day, the blue fleece said to Mum and Dad to call and check, but that they should be able to come and take me home on the 9th of May, which was in 3 days, as I was 'booked in' for tomorrow.

OMG! I was going home in just 3 days' time! I was ecstatic and immediately went into w.b mode and was just on the verge of escalating to the snake, when I suddenly froze…

'Er, booked in for what exactly?'

Chapter 6

WHAT, NO BREAKFAST?!

The next morning, I woke up feeling glad to be alive and full of the joys of spring, well summer actually. In a couple more days, I would be lapping up the benefits of my new home with my new pack. I imagined what I would be doing in 2 days at around this time. I decided that I would probably be tucking in to a scrummy breakfast and then retiring to the sofa, or even Mum and Dad's bed for a little pre-lunch snooze.

Talking of breakfast, where the hell was it today? Aha, I heard the S.D.M wheels approaching in the distance right on cue. I decided that I would just chill out and enjoy my last few days in my room. I was really very fond of my room as it had been my safe sanctuary for the last two weeks. Everyone had been so kind to me and I would never forget them. There was no need to stress over trying to impress potential families any more (though I still always made a fuss of anyone passing of course), I had cracked it. I was 2 more days away from my new life. I had nothing to worry about.

The S.D.M had arrived at last. I was exceptionally hungry due to all the fantasising and daydreaming I had been doing about my new life and I was looking forward to a hearty breakfast. It was my turn next and I had started to drool in anticipation (another one of my embarrassing automatic bodily reactions that I have absolutely no control over), when the unthinkable happened. I watched in total horror as the beloved S.D.M trundled past. I felt panic rising within me and was on the verge of a whimper.

I sent out a frantic, urgent telepathic message to the blue fleece. Er, excuse me……please…..er,….can I have my breakfast?..... Er….hello…..coooeee….over here……please don't go, hey! Don't forget me!........ Er……HEY!………Oh Noooooo!……She forgot to feed me!

I was stunned to be honest. She had just ignored me completely. This had never happened before. Had I done something wrong? Was I getting fat and had been put on a diet? I glanced at my belly, nope; you could still play a tune on my ribs. What on earth was going on?

My day had started so well too. For some reason, I had been denied my breakfast. Well at least it couldn't get any worse than that! Then I remembered that I had been 'booked in' for today. Could this be something to do with being deprived of my beloved brekkie? Then it dawned on me. Of course, why hadn't I thought of it before? I must be booked in to receive a special leaving surprise slap up celebration meal today!

I quickly retired to my blanket, drooling profusely over everything in my path, to eagerly await my lovely surprise.

I didn't have long to wait……

Chapter 7

HAPPINESS HAS ITS PRICE

Soon after breakfast, that I didn't get to have, the blue fleece came to collect me and take me for my surprise. I was quite excited as I still wasn't sure what I was going to get and the mystery deepened as we seemed to be heading towards the clinic.

Maybe it really was a surprise, farewell/good luck party? I had become quite pally with the gorgeous Mastiff girl in my block (I used to like my girls big till I met Speck) and I was hoping that she would be there to give me a fond farewell slobber. I hoped that she would soon find a nice family to take her home too. All dogs deserve a second chance of happiness and it seemed that I, lucky boy that I was, was no exception. I had bagged myself a new life and now my friends would be waiting there in the clinic to shower me with good luck wishes, wags and slobbers. I hoped that nobody would cry. I hoped that I wouldn't cry! I was starting to feel a bit emotional and was trying my best to prepare and re-arrange my face and ears into a bemused, surprised, taken aback expression, ready for seeing them all standing there waiting for me when the door opened.

The door swung open and, SURPRISE!... There were no rows of sad 'I am going to miss you' faces. There was just the head nurse and the vet. Maybe it was a fancy dress party as they were wearing hats and masks and rubber gloves. What was going on here?

Nobody told me what was happening and for some reason, the nurse started to shave my legs; well one of them anyway, but then she seemed to change her mind and just did a little patch. She wiped the bald patch with some smelly stuff and then to my horror, I was gripped in a bear hold and was having my leg squeezed. This was some crazy party. Then, they stuck a sharp needle into my leg and within seconds, I was out like a light. Sparko, zonked. Just like that.

I don't know how long I had been asleep, but when I woke up, I was in a small room in the clinic, all on my own. I must have fallen asleep and missed my own party! My brain was very foggy, but I was gradually starting to remember what happened. I fell asleep immediately after the nurse stuck a needle in my leg. Why did she do that? It wasn't very kind of her. I had always been very polite and waggy to her.

My mouth felt very sore and it tasted of blood. My tongue was all dry and crusty where it had been hanging out of my mouth while I was asleep. It was stuck to the floor, so I slowly peeled it off of the lino and drew it back into my mouth for some vital re-hydration and noticed that it didn't hurt when it touched my rotten tooth. It didn't hurt, because the rotten tooth was no longer there. Aha! That was it!

They had made me go to sleep so that they could remove that manky molar for me, how nice of them. I was feeling very muzzy headed and thought that maybe if I stood up and had a walk around, I would feel a bit better so I scrabbled around trying to get up, but my leg to brain co-ordination left a lot to be desired. I was sliding around and doing the splits like Bambi on the ice (I love that film).

All of a sudden, I felt a sharp twinge in the area of my 'nether regions', so thought I'd better have a little look and investigate to see what on earth was going on down there.

AAAAGH!!!! Where the hell did they go?! Someone had stolen my puppy making equipment while I was asleep! This was one weird party I would never forget.

I was very groggy for the rest of the day and felt extremely sorry for myself. I didn't even feel up to my dinner and that had never ever happened before.

I could understand why the manky tooth was missing, and I was grateful that it was gone, but for the life of me I couldn't work out who had stolen my assets and why?

The next day, I was still very sore in 'the downstairs department', but I ate a little of my breakfast and managed to waddle outside for a quick wee. Ow, Ow OUCH! Bit stingy!

Do you know, not only had someone stolen my bits, but they had also practiced their sewing skills on me too! The stitches pulled when I walked, so I didn't feel up to going far.

While I was out, I managed to have a quick chat to my lovely Mastiff lady friend and despite my obvious embarrassment, I told her of my dreadful plight. She was very sympathetic and understanding. She was a lovely gal and to my shame, I had a brief, but wonderful vision of what might have been, had my bits not been stolen. They would have been beautiful puppies.

She told me that tragically, I was just the latest inmate to fall victim to the dreaded 'Battersea Serial Bits Snatcher'. Apparently, the very same thing had happened to many other dogs just before they were due to leave the kennels to start their new lives. How very odd.

We wished each other luck and had a lovely fond farewell slobber, and then I slowly and painfully tottered back to my room.

As I lay there, with an inferno raging between my back legs, I was desperately trying to remember exactly what had happened at the clinic and figure out why anyone would want to steal my bits.

I could find no logical answer, but one thing I had concluded after hearing that news from my Mastiff girl, was that this was no coincidence………..

Happiness, it seems, has its price!

Chapter 8

GOING HOME!

The next morning I awoke feeling a lot happier. The inferno down below had died down overnight to a mild flickering of embers and it was the long awaited day that I was going home to start my new life.

I virtually pounced on my breakfast - a sure sign that I was on the mend and then paced around wondering what time my new Mum and Dad would collect me. After a couple of hours, I began to wonder if I had the wrong day, or worse still, that they had changed their minds. I started to panic, so quickly forced myself to lie down and chill out. I had to try to remain calm, otherwise by the time they did come to get me, I would be a saucer-eyed, uncontrollable, hyper-hound, bouncing off the walls and squealing with excitement. I probably wouldn't even make it to the car park before being taken back to my room and put up for re-homing again. So I thought calm thoughts and eventually dozed off, dreaming of the wonderful experiences soon to come my way.

I hadn't slept properly since my bits had been stolen. After that horrific event, I always kept one eye half open and one ear cocked just in case. I didn't want to lose any more vital body parts!

At last, the nice blue fleece arrived and announced that my new Mum and Dad were here to take me home. Now that the moment had come, I couldn't believe that it was really happening for me.

Maybe I was still asleep and dreaming again? I got up and shook myself. Ow! Stitches pulling. Nope, I was definitely awake.

Mum and Dad were asked to come up to meet me outside the kennel block, because I was scared stiff of going up and down the big marble steps from the kennel block to reception and refused point blank to even put one paw on that slippery surface.

I had a severe phobia about hard, shiny floors. Laminates, tiles and marble would just fill me with terror. I felt so unsafe walking on them and with giraffe legs like mine, they are hard enough to co-ordinate and control at the best of times, so carpet or a rough surface to grip my toenails into was always a must for me.

I was a bit slower than usual, due to my recent 'asset theft', but I eventually got to the exit, and there they were! They were all smiley and happy to see me, ME, their new pack member! The old tail started to do its thing, and was fast approaching windmillbutt, so I very carefully sat down to stop it. I'm not sure what was more uncomfortable, the rotating tail, or sitting down. Both were quite painful, but at least I had prevented the snake from making an appearance. My stitches would almost certainly have popped out!

There was a lot of talking going on, and I picked out a few things I had to have, like more of those anti-biwhatsit pills, stitches coming out (thank god for that!) and something about micro-chipping, whatever that was. Sounded like something nice like maybe small chips or crisps? Then I heard talk of me going to the clinic to have it done there and then and my heart sank.

Whenever I had been to the clinic, although the people were lovely as most people are, something painful had happened to me. I couldn't help having this awful feeling that micro-chipping was probably not something nice at all, but something else that was going to hurt.

Mum and Dad walked me slowly over to the clinic, and were excitedly chattering away and patting me all the time, but I just couldn't enjoy the moment for worrying what dreadful torture I was about to receive at the clinic.

When we arrived, the nurse came to get me and loudly announced to Mum and Dad that I would almost certainly scream the place down, as all Lurchers and Greyhounds are big wimps. Oh how charming! I was really quite hurt by this remark and decided that no matter how terrible this micro-chipping torture was and no matter how much I wanted to cry and howl, I would not allow myself to let my breed down. I would show them that we are not all big wimps and that we are very brave and courageous at all times.

I was led into the dreaded room. My legs had started to tremble and I could hear rustling noises as the nurse prepared her terrible instruments of torture.

I decided not to look and shut my eyes tight.

The nurse got hold of my scruff and I felt a sharp sting for a second, but it all happened so quickly, that

I didn't even get time to cry. Was that it? Was that the micro-chipping thingy all over and done with? Yes, it seemed so, as the nurse made a big fuss of me and told me I was a very good boy.

With that, she took me back to Mum and Dad and said in a very loud voice: "I was surprised, but he didn't make any fuss, he was a very brave boy!" I was so proud of myself, that I dispensed slobbers all round and had to sit on my tail again before it got too carried away in the moment.

There was some paperwork changing hands and more talk of me coming back for the stitches to be removed. I found out that I had to have more of the anti-biwhatsits because my wound was a bit sore. They also gave Mum a big plastic funnel thing to stop me cleaning the stitches too much. Wasn't sure what that was all about at the time, but I found out later.

Oh yeah, just call me 'Funnel face!'

The next thing I knew, Dad was lifting me into MY car. I sniffed around and was delighted to find that I had a lovely duvet to lie on. I sat there, nose in the air, feeling like I was a million dollar top dog. Then a horrible thought crossed my mind. 'Please God; don't let me throw up all over my lovely duvet and my lovely car and my lovely new Mum and Dad!'

As Dad drove us away, I looked back at the kennels and those lovely people that had cared for me so well (except for when they stole my assets of course) and I vowed never to forget them all. But for now, my mind was elsewhere, because today was the 9th of May and I was GOING HOME!

Chapter 9

HOME SWEET HOME

Mum was sitting in the back of the car with me, and she explained that we would stop off just for a few minutes on the way home, MY HOME! to introduce me to the people that she worked with, as I might occasionally get to spend a day there with her.

As we went along, I was trying to look everywhere at the same time and was almost giving myself whiplash. It was all so exciting! Normally, I was in a dark van with no windows, but in MY car, I could see everything! Mum had opened the windows and both sunroofs (I have two in my car) and the combination of fresh air, new sniffs wafting in and so much to look at, was taking my mind off of my 'delicate tummy problem' and I soon arrived at Mum's place of work, all clean and thankfully NOT wearing this morning's partially digested breakfast, complete with carrots.

Mum took me inside and I was introduced to everyone. There were only two people there, but that was almost everyone. It was a very small company she worked for.

It was there that I had my first of many encounters with a terrifying 'wooden hill'. After much coaxing and tugging, I shakily made it to the top and into another room, where Mum said that she sat every day to do her work. We only stayed for a few minutes, then after much bribing, coaxing and tugging to get me back down the wooden hill, we said our farewells and got back into my car.

Man that wooden hill was so scary, but I was proud of myself for surviving it and Mum and Dad were very proud of me too.

We had only been back in the car and driving along for a few minutes, when we parked up outside a small white house.

"This, Sonic my boy", said Dad, "Is your new home!"

Dad helped me out of the car again and I stood looking at MY house.

So this was it then. Home Sweet Home!

Chapter 10

A LOT TO LEARN

As Mum opened the front door to my new home, my ears were assaulted by strange cheeps and squawks coming from within. What on earth was in there? I was already a bit nervous at stepping inside my new home for the very first time without all that awful racket adding to my angst.

I cautiously put one paw over the threshold and shakily followed with the second, then the third and fourth, then came the tail, which was for once, quite unsure of itself and was doing its best to hide under my belly. Then, at last, I was standing inside my new home for the very first time.

My nose was immediately bombarded with an assortment of alien smells, which I couldn't quite identify. The scent messages were rapidly transmitted to the old brain box, which was frantically trying to decipher, analyse and make sense of them. They were all a bit of a confusing jumble, but I managed to single out one that was very familiar. I could definitely smell feathers, but they smelt a bit odd. Not like the usual pigeons and starlings that I enjoyed chasing round the park, but there were birds in there somewhere. I suspected that's what was making all the noise.

As I was led into the first room, my suspicions were confirmed, as there, in their own little houses with bars, were the strangest looking pigeons I had ever seen.

They were all different colours, but they all had weird flat beaks, like they had flown face first into a wall or something. The small ones had funny little tufty hats on. I was very excited and immediately threw myself at the nearest one, hoping that it would fly out of its house so that I could chase it.

I had forgotten that Mum was on the other end of the lead. She shouted "NO!" and tugged at the same time. I sort of went upwards and backwards and ended up twisting round in mid-air, landing flat on my butt facing her, feeling very hurt and confused. Landing on my butt with a thud had not done my wound any favours and my sore bits were protesting painfully. She waggled a finger at me and sternly told me that the birds were NOT my toys. They were important members of my pack and that under no circumstances must I touch them, scare them, or harm them in any way. I must learn to respect them as this was their home too and they were there first.

I was a little upset at having been told off after just 30 seconds of arriving in my new home, but I accepted that I had no manners, no idea of right from wrong or how to behave in a home and therefore, I had to learn by my mistakes. Mum then explained that it wasn't my fault and she wasn't actually cross with me at all, but she would have to tell me when I was doing something wrong, so that I would learn the 'house rules' and we could all live happily together.

I had learnt lesson No.1: THE BIRDS WERE NOT MY TOYS AND WERE STRICTLY OFF LIMITS TO ME.

After the embarrassing bird incident, something wonderful happened. I walked through into the next room and there, in all its glory, bathed in a halo of serene light was **MY FOREVER SOFA!**
I tested it for comfort with one front paw and it was just as lovely and comfy as I had hoped it would be. I was so looking forward to giving it a full 'test drive' and was about to clamber up for a long awaited sprawl, when Mum said "plenty of time for a snooze later Sonic, come on lets show you the rest of your new home first". I was a little miffed, but she had a point, there were a lot more exciting things to see, sniff and taste.
I was taken out to explore my new garden and allowed as much time as I wanted to sniff around. If my nostrils weren't deceiving me, there had been cats, hedgehogs and slime monsters roaming around. I was definitely going to like it here. I decided to announce my presence and ownership of the turf by peeing up the fence and to my amazement and joy, Mum rushed over and made a huge fuss of me, like I had just won a big race or something. I had no idea why I had been awarded such sudden praise, but of course I accepted it graciously and returned the compliment with a slobbery kiss on her nose, which she seemed to enjoy.

After a while, I decided to go back inside and explore the rest of my home. I spent a good hour sniffing and tasting everything.

Mum and Dad watched with amusement as I gently mouthed the door handles, chair legs and pretty much everything really, except the birds of course. I steered well clear of them! I think that Mum and Dad thought it was cute and that I was doing this just because I had never seen these things before in my life. Of course, this was true, but the main reason was to check out for future reference what was edible and what was not!

I was relieved to find that there were no horrible, slippery, scary floors to negotiate and although there was a wooden hill leading to more rooms upstairs, it was lined with carpet material, so if I was expected to climb up and down it later, at least I could dig my toenails in for a bit of extra security and comfort.

After thoroughly exploring every inch of the ground floor of my new home, I decided that although it was all a bit strange and scary, it was very comfy and satisfactory. I was very pleased with it and decided to proclaim my ownership to all. I was in the process of raising my back leg to perform the deed, when Mum and Dad simultaneously shouted a resounding "NO!" I was precariously balanced on 3 legs and was so taken aback that I almost toppled over. I was then swiftly bundled back out into the garden.

I had learnt lesson No.2: NO PEEING INDOORS!

I love toys. I mean I really and truly LURVE toys.

In the kennels, we were given toys, but they were taken away regularly to be washed along with our bedding and were replaced with different ones. I don't want to sound ungrateful or anything and I know it was for our own good so that we didn't get any germs, but I found this a little upsetting.

You see, at the risk of you thinking me a bit of a soppy old pansy, I will admit that one of my many endearing little quirks, is that I get very attached to my toys. All of my toys are cherished and played with and I can become quite distressed when one of them goes missing.

I'll let you into a little secret here. I would point blank refuse to go to bed without Teds. Teds is my much loved night time bear that Aunty Debs and Uncle Dan bought me. These days, I am much less obsessive with my toys, but back then in the early days, they were a very big obsession in my life and second only to dinner.

Mum reckons it's because I never had anything of my own before. I reckon she could be right.

My toy obsession had escalated into a bit of a problem, in that I didn't like Mum and Dad touching them, any of them. I was so afraid that they might take them away and that I wouldn't get them back again.

Of course, they were only taking them to throw for me to fetch, but as with any obsessive behavioural problem, logic went out of the window and panic rapidly set in each time they went to take one of my toys. I actually got so distressed that I am ashamed to say, I would start to growl. Of course I would never hurt either of them, I just didn't want them to take my toy, so I tried to tell them in my own way. Mum told me that although she understood why I was behaving in this way, it was unacceptable behaviour, especially as there were little people in the family and I might scare them. She said that this must be 'nipped in the bud' and so my mini therapy sessions began. I was persuaded to hand over my toy without any fuss in exchange for a treat or a different toy.

If I growled, I was totally ignored for a while. I found this even more upsetting than having my toy taken away. If I let Mum take my toy from me without grumbling, I would get a huge fuss and a treat and the toy was immediately returned to me.

Once I realised that I got huge fusses if I didn't growl and that my toys would always be coming back anyway, I relaxed and stopped having the panic attacks whenever anyone touched them. I was cured!

I had learnt lesson No.3: ALWAYS SHARE YOUR POSESSIONS AND NEVER GROWL AT YOUR FELLOW PACK MEMBERS.

I had a lovely afternoon exploring and getting to know my new home. It was all very bewildering, but also exciting at the same time, sort of like landing on a different planet. Everything was completely alien, but it was really wonderful sampling all of the new sights, sounds and smells.

There was a big conifer tree in my new garden, with lots of low branches that were just the right height for comfortable chewing. I had gone back out there and was enjoying gnawing my way through my second branch, when Mum called me in for lunch. Obviously I didn't need calling twice and made short work of it. Even the old anti-biwhatsit pill went down a treat.

Moving into a new home is very appetite-building you know.

After my lovely meal, I flopped out on the floor by Mum and Dad's feet. I wanted to lie on my 'forever sofa', but I wanted to stay with them even more, so opted for the carpet. The sofa would be there forever after all, so plenty of time to lay on it.

While I was stretched out on the floor, I noticed, for the first time (funny how you miss stuff at first when there's so much exciting stuff to see), the large tree trunk on legs right in front of me. It had cups and other weird stuff perched on top of it.

I decided to carry on where I left off earlier in the garden and had just sunk my teeth into a corner of it, when there was another resounding "NO!"

I had learnt lesson No.4: I WAS ONLY ALLOWED TO EAT WOOD THAT WAS IN THE GARDEN. INDOOR WOOD WAS CALLED FURNITURE AND WAS NOT TO BE CONSUMED.

I had been laying down for a while, when I became aware of a very annoying, itchy, tingly sensation where my stitches were, so I thought I would cover them with saliva to sooth the awful itch, but that made it worse. It was driving me mad and I started to get quite stressed so I decided that I would bite the evil things out. That would solve the problem.

All of a sudden, Mum appeared from out of nowhere, wielding that plastic funnel thing that they gave her at the clinic. She stuck it over my head and said "sorry boy, but it's for your own good". How the hell did she figure that one out?! Those stitches were driving me insane and she sticks a funnel on my head so that I can't nibble them out!

I had learnt lesson No.5: NEVER EVER TRY TO UNDERSTAND HUMAN LOGIC.

Dad got up and went into the kitchen and Mum got up and walked over to the TV box. I went over to see what she was doing, and the box suddenly lit up and came alive. It was very noisy and I was scared half to death, so I ran away to hide under my duvet. Mum came and found me and persuaded me to come back in and sit with her. She had made it quieter, so it wasn't as scary and after a while, I felt brave enough to go over to sniff it. I had almost got my nose on it, when the big scary cat that was in the box, suddenly charged towards me.

As I mentioned earlier, I am really quite scared of cats and this was no little pussycat. It was a big African one with huge teeth and claws and it was coming right at me roaring its big scary head off!

It was all a bit too much for me and I scurried back to hide under my duvet again.

Eventually, I was coaxed back out again with a biscuit and a fuss and Mum went over to the TV box and said "Look Sonic, see, it's ok" and she tapped it.

I was embarrassed but relieved to see that there was a hard cover on the front keeping everything safely inside.

I had learnt lesson No 6: SCARY THINGS IN THE TV BOX CANNOT JUMP OUT AND EAT YOU.

It was soon time for my first walk around my new neighbourhood and I couldn't wait to meet the natives and sniff the sniffs. Off we went, all three of us (the birds stayed at home I'm very pleased to say). I was chuffed to bits. I was walking out with my new pack, on my new turf. I was still a bit sore down under, but did my best to strut my stuff and look handsome and impressive, just in case we bumped into any of the locals. First impressions are very important to us hounds you know. I didn't want my street cred in tatters because I'd been seen by the local hard mutt, walking like I had two red hot house bricks strapped between my back legs.

It was a good walk, full of great new sniffs and I even got a few fusses along the way.

I spotted a few of the local hounds, but wasn't near enough to introduce myself. Oh well, it was only my first day. There would be plenty of other walks and time for making acquaintances.

On our way back, I spotted a tiny white kitten sitting in a gateway. We locked eyes, and to my horror, this tiny scrap of a cat started calling to me and then came trotting over. I couldn't quite believe the cheek of it. I was doing my best to look ferocious and unapproachable, but it obviously wasn't fooled by my act, as it continued to advance, meowing loudly.

I anxiously looked up at Mum and Dad for help and protection, but they seemed to think that it was cute. As it came up to me, I shut my eyes, waiting for a swipe across the nose with razor sharp talons, but it rubbed its fluffy little body all around my legs and was making a noise a bit like a bumble bee trapped in an empty drink bottle.

I opened my eyes and looked down at it and it meowed in my face. Pooh, disgusting fish breath! He was a cute little guy all the same and I couldn't stop myself from lying down on the path at his level to give him a fuss.

I was in mid slobber, when I happened to notice that I was being observed from across the road, by one of the biggest, meanest looking dogs I have ever seen. Oh great! I had been seen by the local hard mutt, unashamedly slobbering over a cute little baby cat in broad daylight, in public, in the middle of the street. My street cred was in tatters.

I had learnt Lesson No.7: ALWAYS MAKE SURE THAT THE COAST IS CLEAR BEFORE DISPLAYING AFFECTION TO A CAT IN PUBLIC, ESPECIALLY A CUTE BABY CAT!

I finished making a fuss of Tiddles, as there was no point in rushing off. The damage was already done and it wasn't his fault. He was only a titchy puss and besides, I was secretly enjoying it too. I had made my first true friend in my new neighbourhood and it was a baby cat! We said our farewells and I headed off home. HOME! I really liked the sound of that!

I spent the next few hours playing, being fussed and making short work of a very yummy dinner and then it was bed time. I went outside for a wee (see, I learn quickly) and wondered where I would be sleeping. When I came in, Dad made a fuss of me then locked the door and Mum suddenly advanced brandishing a weird little brush. "it's teethy time!", she announced and promptly lifted up my lips and started to scrub my gnashers with the brush. I had no idea what this strange behaviour was in aid of, but it seemed to make her happy and there was some quite nice tasting stuff coated on the brush, so I went along with it without making too much fuss. I even quite enjoyed it once I got used to the funny scrubbing sensation and tried to chew the tasty brush, which Mum wasn't so happy about. After several minutes of her trying to scrub and me trying to chew, she said "Oh I give up"! She gave me a big fuss and then went to wash the brush under the tap. This was to be a regular, nightly fiasco.

Dad, who had been watching and laughing his head off at our 'teethy time' antics, said "come on boy, up to bed". UP to bed? OMG! I realised that I was going to have to negotiate the scary wooden hill.

After much coaxing, tugging and shoving, I was at the top and soon sprawled out on my lovely comfy duvet on the floor next to Mum and Dad's bed. I did intend to wait till they had gone to sleep and then creep up on their bed with them, but I'd had such an exhausting day, that I was well and truly sparko as soon as my head hit the pillow (yes, I actually do have a pillow!).

It had been an exciting, but exhausting first day in my new home. I still had an awful lot to learn, but Mum and Dad said that I had done very well and that they were very proud of me.

I learnt a lot of important lessons on my first day at home and have learnt many more since, but the most valuable lesson I learnt that day, was the last one, as I eventually succeeded in climbing up the wooden hill.

I had learnt Lesson No.8: TO CONQUER YOUR FEARS, YOU FIRST HAVE TO FACE THEM.

Chapter 11

RUDE AWAKENING

I was smack bang in the middle of a great dream where I was in hot pursuit of a huge chunk of roast beef on legs, running across a field of soft grass, when I was rudely awakened by music coming from somewhere in the room. Dad sleepily clambered out of bed and almost trod on my face. He apologised and gave me a fuss and thankfully shut the music up.

He staggered out to the bathroom and I was just snuggling back under my duvet, about to resume the chasing down of my dinner, when he re-appeared and threw open the curtains. Both me and Mum whimpered and recoiled under our respective duvets trying to protect our delicate retinas from the blinding daylight, but Dad pulled my duvet off of me and said "c'mon boy, we gotta go to work!"

WHAT?! I was mortified. I am a Lurcher. I was born containing the lazy gene. We do not do work! I didn't remember ever agreeing to be an employee. I was supposed to be a pet for goodness sake! There must have been some mistake. He must be winding me up. I soon realised that it was no wind up. I really did have a job to go to.

I used to make a big effort in the kennels, but I really don't do mornings very well at all. Oh well, I decided that I ought to give it a go to keep Dad happy. If I didn't like it, I could always resign I suppose.

Dad explained that I would be going to work with him every day, but might have to go with Mum on the odd day that he couldn't take me with him.

So, I was going to be a 9-5 working dog!

He told me that he spent part of his day in the office and part in the workshop. He said that I would have my duvet in his office. I wondered what my job title would be… Maybe Pest Control Officer? (I was a whizz at catching and eating flies and moths). Or Head of Security? Wow! Yes, that was it, I was going to be a Guard dog! If anybody came into Dad's office, I would whip them with my psychotic tail and slobber them into submission!

Dad told me that their usual Office Hound, called Diggit (Diggie to his friends), had just taken early retirement. He lived with his Nanny Sylvia, Monica and Michele. Michele was the Office Manager.

Mum loved Diggie to bits and often used to borrow him to take for walks around Burnham Beeches.

I eventually got to meet Diggie and we became really good pals. He was an ex-Battersea boy too, so we had lots in common. He was at Battersea for 18 months until Michele and Monica took him home. Diggie was a Staffie and was badly scarred, which had sadly put people off, but the poor boy was almost certainly used as a 'bait dog' and not a fighter, as he was so good natured and scared of other Staffie's.

Anyway, it was to be my first day at work, but first I had to get down the wooden hill with a full bladder without breaking my neck and weeing myself!

Chapter 12

RAINING CARROTS

After eventually mastering the wooden hill, just about making it to the garden without disgracing myself and making short work of my first breakfast in my new home, me and Dad gave Mum a goodbye slobber (I got there first) and off we went to earn a crust, or is it win some bread? Anyway, off we went to work.

I was hoping that work was within walking distance, i.e. at the end of the road, but unfortunately, my hopes were dashed when Dad said that I had to get into the car.

I tried hard not to think about the fact that I had only just eaten my breakfast and that there was a very real possibility of getting to eat it again. I looked out of the window and thought pleasant thoughts, but I was a tad nervous about starting my new job and was very much aware of my breakfast slowly rising up towards my throat. I tried swallowing hard and fast and I thought that I had contained it, when the car hit a pothole and there was a sudden and unstoppable rush from the depths of my stomach. I was helpless as I saw my lovely breakfast shoot up in a big arc and splatter all over my front paws, the duvet, the car window, the car seat and just about everywhere in the back of the car.

Looking around me, I thought that things couldn't possibly get any worse and then cringed as I spotted what looked suspiciously like a chunk of slimy carrot nestling in the back of Dad's hair.

Poor Dad soon realised what had happened (though he hadn't yet noticed his carrot hat) and opened all the windows to get some fresh air into the stinky car.

Soon after I had involuntarily despatched my breakfast, we pulled up outside my new workplace.

Dad's first job of the day was going to be cleaning me and the car up. What a fine start to my career!

As we pulled up, I heard excited ladies voices squealing "Where is he then, where is our cute new recruit?!"

Oh no! The ladies, Michele and Carole, my new work colleagues, had come out to welcome me and like when I first arrived at Old Windsor in the back of the Battersea van, I was looking like an abstract modern work of art, painted with brightly coloured splatters of smelly body paint. Literally body paint!

Dad announced that it had been 'raining carrots' in the car and as he opened my door, they all quickly jumped backwards to avoid the stench and the large, gooey globule of my recycled breakfast that was dangling menacingly from the bottom of the door. They were understandably a little disgusted, but must have felt very sorry for the pathetic sight before their eyes, because they made lots of sympathetic noises and promised that they would give me a big fuss once I was vomit free. I decided that I was going to like working here. They were kind ladies, my new work colleagues.

Chapter 13

WORKING 9-5 (my first day at work)

After I had been hosed down and dried off, I was looking and smelling more respectable. I eagerly tugged Dad into the offices so that I could meet my ladies properly and collect my promised fuss and of course administer as many slobbers as I could in return. Dad thoughtfully fed me a mint first to help conceal my vomitty breath!

Despite the earlier 'breakfast disaster', I had a very nice welcoming party in the office and Dad told the ladies all about my first experiences at home. There was lots of fuss and coffee and biscuits (I just had water and one biscuit in case my tummy decided to erupt again) and then it was soon time to start work.

Dad made my bed up in his office, complete with toys and I proudly sat near his desk, watching for any flies or other small intruders that might need chasing off. I was relieved to hear that there were no rodents in the building, as I am scared stiff of rats. Even mice are a bit scary. Flies though, Pah! No probs!

After a while, Dad said that he had to go into his workshop next door to do some 'engineering stuff' and that I was to stay there and be a good boy.

He shut the door and went off to get his paws dirty.

After a few minutes, I decided to have a look around my new office, and being giraffe-like in stature, I can reach pretty much everything.

Dad's desk was rather interesting and had lots of stuff on it that I hadn't seen before. There were loads of bits of paper and cables that were pleasant to chew on and a small, squashy chunk of rubbery stuff, which smelt weird. I was fascinated with this find and just had to have a good old chomp on it. It tasted quite nice and I assumed that it was, in fact, a treat meant for me so I took it to my bed to eat in comfort.

There were also little pull out bits under the desk, which came open easily with a slight tug of my teeth. Some of the things were a bit boring, but the writing things were very nice to play with and even nicer to gnaw on. They made cracking noises when I bit them and were filled with either black solid tasty stuff, or blue runny stuff that tasted ok, but dribbled out all over my paws and bed and onto the carpet too. I especially liked the wooden ones, as they reminded me of chewing on the trees and the furniture at home.

After I had sampled everything on and in the desk, I decided to investigate the contents of the bin in the corner. There were some absolutely amazing finds in there. Mostly there was paper, which, like the paper on the desk, was very nice to shred, but as a bonus, there were a few lumps of hard, but still reasonably tasty chewing gum, welded onto some of them. I knew about chewing gum from when I was living rough. I would find balls of it attached to the underside of park benches where kids had been sitting. I had first found it quite by accident when I was peering under benches one evening looking for slime monsters for my tea. It made a nice change and was quite a challenge to chisel off.

The icing on the cake was literally the icing on the cake. Dad must have had a cake the day before and put the wrapper in the bin. I spent a very happy five minutes licking the last morsels off of the bag and then just in case I had missed any, I decided to eat the whole bag anyway. Well you have to be sure don't you.

I was a little tired after all this and was just about to settle myself down for a little nap, when my nose caught a faint whiff of food. I thought at first that it must be the cake wrapper I had just eaten, but no, it was something else; something savoury!

I went to investigate and found that over in the corner, tucked away, high up on top of another little desk, was a big paper bag. As I got nearer, the savoury smell got stronger and I could hardly believe my luck, as I peered into the bag and saw parcels of food! Some were my biscuits from home and there was bread with delicious smelling ham inside, which must have been for me too.

I was feeling very hungry, especially as my lovely breakfast had been so cruelly snatched away from my poor tum. I decided that I would take the bag over to my bed and help myself to my own food to save Dad time later. Hey, I'm a helpful sort of guy!

Before I started on my biscuits, I thought I might like to have a taste of the bread and ham stuff, just to see what it was like of course.

Several minutes later, lying on my back, feet up in the air (tummy was much too large to lay face down), I was just drifting off into a lovely sleep, when the door creaked open and there peeping round the door, was one of my ladies. She had this really cute look on her face and was just about to go all 'coochey cooey' over me, when she stopped short and looked around my office. Her eyes started to get bigger and her mouth dropped open. She flung the door open wide and shouted very loudly in the direction of Dad's workshop............"GAAARRRREEEEEY!!!"

Dad immediately appeared in the doorway and came into our office. I was very pleased to see him of course and despite the weight of my enormous tum, I made a huge effort and staggered over, all of a wag, to say hello and show him that I had missed him. For some reason, he wasn't too pleased to see me and sharply told me to go back to my bed. He sat on the edge of the desk and looked, quite frankly, very grumpy. I guess he must have had a hard time in the workshop. Good job I had saved him time by feeding myself.

He sighed heavily and ran his fingers through his hair. "What the..?" he said and started tugging at something in his hair. As he sniffed and inspected the smelly, orange chunk, I felt myself automatically sliding underneath my duvet.

After he had finished having some sort of strange seizure, during which he was muttering, twitching and going a funny red colour, he clipped my lead on and dragged me out from under my duvet, past the ladies offices, out the front door and over the road to a nice grass patch, where I gratefully managed to take the pressure off of my poor old overloaded tummy.

He sharply told me I was a good boy, obviously relating to the productive trip to the grass patch, and me helpfully feeding myself earlier, but strangely, was otherwise silent. Poor Dad, he must have been having a really bad day at work. Shame that, because I was having a blast!

For some reason when we got back, Dad dragged my bed out into the corridor and shut our office door. I was a bit confused by this, but then it dawned on me. I was now to guard and protect the corridor leading to all of the 3 offices. Yay! Promotion on my first day!

Dad went out to the shops and bought some food. Do you know, I wish I had saved him one of those bread and ham things as I think he might have liked them. I certainly did!

He went into our office and shut the door. Obviously he wasn't intending to share his food with me, which I thought was a tad selfish of him, but I didn't really mind. I was still stuffed anyway.

Dad came out a little later and told me that he was going back to his workshop, and that I must be a GOOD BOY. I don't know why he said that bit extra loudly. I had been a very good boy so far. I decided not to fret about it, or attempt to understand why he used that tone with me, so I curled up for a nice nap.

Later during the afternoon, I dutifully patrolled the premises and frequently visited my ladies offices.

On my rounds, I found a few more writing things and bits of paper to take to my bed to chew later, in my official break of course. I wasn't about to skive on my first day in my new job. Maybe on the second day it would be acceptable!

I also checked out my ladies bins when they popped out to the loo and I found a few more tasty food wrappers. On one of their desks, I found a huge banana. I had just sunk my teeth into the end of it and was sliding it along the desk towards me, when the lady appeared and squealed and made me jump. I dropped it in surprise and she picked it up and put it in the pull out bit underneath the desk. No worries, I would go back and get it later.

Soon it was break time and everyone sat around the table in the big office drinking tea or coffee (I had water of course) and there was a lot of laughing. Dad had cheered up a lot, which was nice to see. They were definitely discussing me, as they kept looking at me and I picked up little keywords and snippets of the conversation, such as:-

Cheeky, loveable, very friendly, affectionate, funny, loving, a very nice looking boy, handsome, very tall, gorgeous, clever, intelligent, really likes bananas, cakes, ham sarnies, paper, rubbers and pencils.

Then they obviously went on to discuss someone else because I was picking up dreadful things like:-

Needs to learn some manners, very naughty, very crafty, sneaky, greedy gannet, hooligan, vandal, we should sack him!

I don't know what poor soul they were talking about then, but I started to feel a bit sorry for him, as it sounded like he might well lose his job.

I, on the other paw, was already an accepted and valued member of the team. It was only my first day and I had been promoted and the ladies absolutely loved me and who could blame them?

It was Friday and we apparently didn't work for the next two days, as it was 'the weekend', so we said "goodbye, and seeya Monday" to the ladies and got into the car.

We were about halfway home when I felt that awful familiar feeling of churning in the pit of my stomach.

I quickly swallowed hard and fast, but as you know, as with my tail, I have absolutely no control over my stomach mechanism and it was raining carrots (and works stationary) once more. I had very quickly aimed downwards this time though, so Dad wasn't pebble dashed again.

I was such a thoughtful, good boy!

Chapter 14

WEEKENDS ARE GREAT!

It was Saturday morning and we had 2 days off work to play, eat and sleep. My first weekend in my new home! It was around 9am and as I yawned, stretched, and re-arranged myself amongst my very comfy duvet, I sleepily began to think about stuff............

As much as I enjoyed my new job, this weekend thing was just pure bliss and I wondered at what age working dogs retired. I knew that Greyhounds retired at around 4, or sooner if they were a bit on the slow side, but what about us white collared office workers? Diggie had retired early from his office job, to start his new career, which was 'Full Time Companion' for his Nanny Sylvia, but I didn't know any other office hounds to ask.

Dad got up to go down the wooden hill, apparently to make tea and breakfast. Oh how lovely, breakfast in bed. I was just imagining him coming up the stairs with a plate of biscuits for me and a cup of tea for Mum, when he said "c'mon Sonic, up you get boy, down those stairs for wees and breakfast". Charming, they get their breakfast in bed and I have to go down to the kitchen for mine. I could see that I was going to have to work on them over this issue.

I grudgingly left the warmth of my bed and plodded off down the wooden hill to the kitchen. Dad said "wees before brekkie Sonic", so I obediently padded over to the back door.

As I sleepily stared up the garden and started to pee, I was snapped wide awake by Dad shouting" NO!" I realised too late, that he hadn't actually opened the back door yet and although I could clearly see up the garden, I was actually still standing indoors on the mat, looking out through the glass. Oops! Well, I had the right idea and I was still half asleep. I would make a mental note to be more careful tomorrow morning.

I quickly went to finish my pee in the garden and then rushed back in for my breakfast. I had wheaty brick things with milky water, which I wasn't overly keen on, but it was food and I was hungry.

I had a bit of a tummy ache, so I asked to go back outside and just made it to the grass as my back end exploded, or that's how it felt anyway. I guess the excitement of my new home and learning all this new stuff had taken its toll on my tummy. I had also found a couple of those 'slime-monsters' in the garden the night before and couldn't resist sneakily scoffing them as a little late night snack, just for old time's sake.

I used to get an upset tummy a lot when I was living rough, so I think my slimy snack had contributed towards my 'fire belly' that morning.

Dad took breakfast and tea on a tray, up the wooden hill for him and Mum and I rushed back up (I was getting better with practice), to resume my lie in too. As a special treat, I was allowed up on their bed and as I snuggled down in between them, I knew without any doubt, that I had landed on my paws at last!

After a while, we all got up and went down the hill, where I patiently waited on the sofa for lunch time. Mum and Dad were bustling about doing things they called 'household chores'. It all looked too much like hard work from where I was laying and I wondered why on earth people used so much of their precious time and energy doing these strange things, when they could be spending their time relaxing like me. Humans are such odd creatures.

Lunch time came round at last and I was first in line. Within minutes of finishing my meal, I had a bad tummy pain again and had to dash to the garden. I heard Mum say that if it carried on, I would have to see the vet.

I remembered what happened last time I saw 'the vet'!

Later on that day, I had to get into the car as we were driving to the woods for a nice walkies and the old trouble reared its ugly head.

By the time we got there, my lunch (carrots too of course) was evenly distributed all over my paws and my blanket. I wondered if I would ever be able to get into a car without losing my last meal.

After a few minutes out in the fresh air, I started to enjoy our lovely walk. I could smell rabbits and squirrels, but was unable to go and chase them because spoilsport Mum kept me on my lead. Still, it was lovely walking out with my new pack and I met several other dogs out with their respective packs too.

There were two large ponds in the woods, with noisy ducks, clamouring and jostling for bread that people were throwing in for them. I tugged Mum towards the bread, but she thought I was trying to eat the ducks and quickly pulled me the other way. Oh well, it would soon be tea time I suppose.

All too soon it was time to go home, and I had to jump back into the car. I grudgingly got in and laid down, trying to think positive, non vomitty thoughts. I needn't have worried though, because there was nothing left in my tummy to come up. Not even any carrots. I was frothing at the mouth a bit by the time we got back home. I must have looked like that poor Cujo chap that I had seen on the TV box earlier, before Mum turned it off so I didn't get scared.

Something exciting, but very scary happened later that same afternoon. I met next door's cat. She had been cheekily using my garden as a short cut and a toilet. I know that you humans think it is a disgusting habit, but I must admit that eating cat poo is rather enjoyable and a good source of protein.

Mum caught me chewing on one and almost lost her last meal!

Anyway, here's what happened………

On my first day in my new home, I had claimed and ear-marked the concrete area at the end of the garden to be my own personal sunbathing patch.

So, on the Saturday, as I was off work and it was hot and sunny, I decided to go and catch some rays. I was happily sauntering up the garden to stretch out on my concrete patch, when I was horrified and infuriated to see a black furball sitting right in the middle of it! Bold as brass, there it was, sitting on MY sunbathing patch!

It looked at me so I stopped and glared at it, giving it a fair chance to get lost, but it had the audacity to just sit there blatantly glaring back at me, with obviously no intention of giving up its false claim on MY patch. I couldn't let this go, that furball had to be shown just who was in charge here, so I lowered myself down into stalking position and like a lion about to charge his prey, I commenced the stalking procedure.

As I got nearer, I realised that this tactic was not working, so I decided to go with the full on charge assault. As I broke into a high speed gallop, the cat slowly began to move. Ah ha! I had it worried now! As I got to within a few feet, I realised with horror, that this cat was not going to run and instead, it raised itself up to its full height, eyes like big yellow saucers, its black fur standing up like a loo brush and it started to make this very scary noise, which got louder and more higher pitched, the nearer I got.

For my own safety, I slammed the brakes on and skidded to a halt inches away from the mouth of hell. No, really, it was that terrifying! Its ears were flat against its head, its claws were thrashing about millimetres away from my delicate snout and its teeth were like razor sharp needles. It was making this awful noise like a snake and a rabid Rottweiler being shaken up together in a hessian sack. I was petrified.

I couldn't let the cat see how scared I was, though me shaking uncontrollably from head to tail might have given it a clue, but I stood my ground, and so did she.

For the next few minutes (it seemed like hours), we just stood glaring at each other. It was a stand-off until eventually, we both slowly laid down at the same time, not taking our eyes off of each other for one second. We were almost nose to nose and somehow managed to overcome our differences enough to both get some sunbathing in, though I had to resort to lying on the grass, while SHE had the concrete.

I vowed that next time, I would get there first and she would have to take the grass patch. It was MY garden after all, not hers!

This dispute over the concrete patch raged over the next few weeks and was finally resolved by Dad putting a ruddy great wooden shed on top of it! I was obviously upset at having lost MY sun patch, but I was also secretly quite relieved at not having to confront 'her next door' any more. Although we had sort of developed a bit of mutual respect for each other, I always ended up on the grass and always had to put on the bravado act, because I was secretly terrified of her. The worst thing is, despite my desperate efforts to conceal my true feelings, I think she knew it!

That first weekend flew by all too quickly and it was Monday morning and back to work again before I could say "a pig's ear a day keeps the vet away".

Later that week, Mum and Dad took me back to the kennels and finally, those rotten stitches that had become the bane of my life were removed. It twanged a bit, but felt so much better once they were gone. I sure wouldn't be missing those and wouldn't have to suffer the indignity of wearing a funnel on my head any more.

I said hello to all my blue fleece girls there and made a huge fuss of them. I had missed them all.

I had a home visit from one of my lovely blue fleece ladies a week or so later, which I felt was very kind of her to come and see me. She said that I was looking good and that I seemed happy.

And I really was.

Chapter 15

THE GREAT ESCAPE (not so great actually)

I had decided that office work was actually quite boring, though break times were good. There was a 'little people's' play club at the end of the road, where I sometimes managed to administer a slobber or two if I was lucky and there was a hot dog stall and burger van that always smelt divine.

I also enjoyed visiting my ladies throughout the day, checking out their bins and ridding their offices of flies and spiders, but I longed for something really exciting to happen to liven up the day.

My wish came true half way through the week, when a delivery man had left Dad's workshop doors open.

I had never been in Dad's workshop before, as it was out of bounds, but the door was open and I was curious to see what was in there. I peeped round the door and saw that the double doors were wide open and Dad was outside in the back of a van looking at some boring old boxes.

I was going to trot over to say hello, but was disappointed to see that the floor had a horrible shiny surface, so I shuddered and reversed back into the corridor, keeping my paws firmly planted on the safe, comforting carpet. I was just about to go back to my bed when I heard little people squealing outside and I caught a whiff of the burger van.

The outside world was calling, so I decided to brave the scary, shiny floor and make a run for it.

The floor was even more slippery and terrifying than I expected and it sent me into total panic. I skidded and fell and got to my feet and just kept running until I had no idea where I was.

I thought that I heard Dad calling me in the distance, but by the time I had calmed myself down and stopped running, I couldn't hear him anymore.

I spotted some people across the road and went up to them to ask for help. They made a fuss of me and looked at the I.D tag on my collar. The man started to rummage around in his jacket pocket and I was just getting that pre-salivating tingle in my mouth at the thought of him producing a tasty treat, when the drooling process was stopped in its tracks by the sudden appearance of a mobile phone.

He got his lady friend to read the number out on my tag, which was not easy for her as I was doing my best to snuffle and de-wax her right ear at the same time. I thought that they must be calling Dad to come and get me. The man then said something about "just an answer phone" and with that, they shooed me away and started to walk off.

Obviously I was feeling hurt and confused by this sudden rejection and I knew that I had to find my own way back to work, but I am a Sighthound, not a Scenthound.

Being a Sighthound is useful if you are familiar with your surroundings, or if you are keeping a fleeing furry thing in your sights, but totally useless if you can see the landmarks perfectly well, but don't know where they are in relation to where you need to get to.

I needed a good nose to sniff my way back, but scent work has never been my strong point, unless it involves food of course, then it's second to none, but I was totally out of my depth here.

I began to feel a bit panicky, but gave myself a talking to. I had wanted adventure and here it was. I decided that I was going to make the most of it while I had the chance. I was going to explore this new place and maybe even make a few new friends in the process. I am a Lurcher and therefore an opportunist by gene default. I was going to have fun!

I further raised my spirits by thinking that I might come across other hounds, maybe even a fit girl, or even better, maybe some little people. Or even better still, little people with food!

I was leaning against a wall in the sunshine wondering which way might lead me to magical adventures, when a bus came along and scared me half to death with that terrifying pshhhhhhhhhhh noise they make.

I ran as fast as I could in the opposite direction and ended up in a quiet road with lots of interesting sniffs at every gatepost. This was obviously a favourite road for dogs out walking their humans.

I soon got engrossed in all these new intriguing aromas and spent a pleasant half an hour wandering along collecting fascinating scent information on the local packs that padded down this road.

One scent in particular was especially strong; in fact it was so strong and pongy that it actually made me sneeze. I realised that this was the mark of the local Alpha male and judging by the signals I was picking up, he was one hell of a dog and definitely NOT to be messed with.

I toyed with the idea of peeing over his stamp of authority just to be rebellious, after all, I was now a rebel on the run, so I was entitled to challenge him. My rebellious great escape must surely have boosted my testosterone levels, making my usually subtle, but highly attractive scent (if I do say so myself) much more potent and respect commanding.

Hm 'to pee, or not to pee, that was the question'. After a few minutes, I finally decided that yup, I was gonna go for it! I was going to claim this patch, and let the local girls sniff what a REAL hero smelt like. And I needed to go anyway.

Decision made, I started the serious business of covering the Alpha's stamp with my own. I had to keep stopping in mid flow to ensure that there was enough to go round. I had to do the job properly. I'm very conscientious you know.

I was almost at the end of the road and almost on empty, actually, I was running on fumes by this time, when I started to feel that uncomfortable feeling that someone was staring at me.

My right back leg was aching badly with all that cocking, but I quickly held it up higher and stuck my nose into the air. I felt sure that it must be one of the local lassies that had picked up my irresistible aroma and she was just across the road checking me out.

I was fast running out of fuel, but I decided to act cool and play hard to get, so I held my pose and hoped that she wouldn't actually notice the fuel shortage situation.

The suspense was killing me. I just had to see her, so I raised my lip at one corner of my mouth to expose a few millimetres of dazzling white canines (the girls just can't resist a guy with a good set of gnashers) and coolly turned my head to meet the gaze of my admirer.

My raised leg began to tremble and my lip dropped back down over my pearlies as I stared across the street into the eyes of the biggest, meanest, ugliest looking crossbreed I have ever seen.

He just stood there, motionless, glaring right at me.

There was no expression on his big, battle scarred face and the only outward sign of his inner feelings, was the ridge of fur that was raised up along the length of his huge back.

I felt a surge of fear rising from deep within and shakily lowered my leg. All 4 of them were turning to jelly, when the penny suddenly dropped. Of course! He must be a Ridgeback cross! It wasn't a sign of aggression, it was just the way the poor fellow was put together; he couldn't help it, poor lad. I bet he was a sweetie pie really.

This poor dog was probably terrified of me. He must have noticed my scary scent all along the road, so to reassure him that I meant him no harm, I slowly relaxed my whole body and quickly re-arranged my muzzle into a friendly smile then gave him a little wag and bowed my head.

I was just about to top it all off with a cheesy grin, when I noticed his lips slowly peeling upwards and backwards, revealing the longest, sharpest, pointiest and scariest looking set of fangs I had ever seen in my life! He lunged forwards and broke into a gallop.

Let me tell you, this was one of those rare times when I actually thanked God for my gangly limbs. When I am scared, NOBODY can catch me, though this enraged animal was having a damn good try!

Of course, being the canine equivalent to the cheetah, I had the obvious advantage of speed, but unbeknown to me, my pursuer had the advantage of knowing all the streets and consequently all of the short cuts.

I took off and ran hell for leather down the road and felt sure that I had shaken him off as there was no sign of him when I looked over my shoulder.

I slowed down and came to a halt next to a tree. I was rather hot and welcomed the shade while I got my puff back.

I was feeling pleased with myself for outrunning the thug hound from hell, when from out of nowhere, WHAM! this huge snarling mass of fur, teeth and fury suddenly hit me full on like a train.

All the air had been knocked from my body and as I lay on my back winded and stunned, my eyes slowly came back into focus and I found myself staring right into the most terrifying, rage ravaged, ugly old furry face you could ever imagine. I had never before seen such huge, sharp, but frankly quite disgusting brown fangs.

Now, at this moment in time, the old saying rang true and my life flashed before my eyes. I was saddened at just how dismal and unhappy it had been. I had been privileged to have been given a second chance of a new, happy and safe life with Mum and Dad and I had blown it in one stupid, selfish moment and I vowed that if, by some miracle, I actually survived this day, I would never ever run off in search of adventure again.

As the manky fangs moved in closer and the growling grew more intense, I was suddenly engulfed by toxic gas. Man this hound had a severe case of halitosis! The worst I had ever smelt in my life. Even after I had been cleaning my butt and eating cat poo or a long deceased rabbit, I swear I had never had bog breath that bad! The stench was so overwhelmingly powerful that it activated my sneeze mechanism and my whole body went into uncontrollable contortions. My face must have looked like a bag of hyperactive ferrets on speed.

My attacker was obviously both fascinated and unnerved by his strange looking victim, who was twitching and gurning for England right there before his eyes, and he stopped the scary growling and just stared, open jawed in bewilderment.

All of a sudden, the end product of my facial contortions was explosively released. Yes folks, the hell hound was liberally showered with an impressive amount of Sonic snot, right in the mush! It was dripping from his eyes and ears and he had taken a direct hit in the gob too.

Probably for the first time in his life, this bully boy had met his match. I don't mind betting that he had never before been snotted on with such velocity at such close range and in those few seconds that his old grey matter was trying to decipher what had just happened, my young grey matter took full advantage and I seized my opportunity to escape.

I kicked all 4 limbs upwards as hard as I could. My front paws caught him square on the lower jaw and he flew up in the air and before he knew what had hit him, I was up and away on my paws and was 2 blocks away, probably before he had even picked himself up off of the pavement.

I was still hurtling along at breakneck speed, when my nostrils were hit by the most amazing aroma on this earth. Fried chicken!

I screeched to a halt almost burning my pads off (again) in the process. (I made a mental note to stop doing that because it really hurts!) I reversed a bit and glanced up and there it was, just above the doorway, that familiar bearded man's smiling face, bathed in lights of red and white.

I was just about to go inside and put on my most pathetic, starving looking face, when I felt a hand on my collar. I looked up into the face of a kind man, who stroked me and told me it would be ok. Well it almost was!! This was just my luck. Why couldn't this nice man have come along to rescue me just a few minutes later, AFTER I had eaten my chicken?

He took me across the road to a garage where he said he worked and he looked at my I.D. tag and picked up his phone. I could hear that he was talking to someone and I prayed that it was Mum or Dad and not the dog pound. I had had enough of adventures for one day. I was very hungry and did not ever want to spend another night out on the streets all alone. I had been there and got the T-shirt, as you say.

I had been very lucky to have narrowly escaped the smelly, decaying jaws of death. I might not be so lucky next time if he got hold of me.

All I wanted to do now was see my Mum and Dad and go home.

In a few minutes, I got my wish and Mum and Dad pulled up in the car and rushed over. I was so relieved to see them again and was actually keen to get in the car for once.

Mum and Dad thanked the nice man and I gave him a lovely thank you slobber, and off we went. I was exhausted and just wanted to go home, but as it wasn't yet 5 o'clock, I had to go back to work, where I slept soundly until home time; though I did have a nasty dream about huge sets of stinky brown fangs snapping at my throat!

Boring as it may have been, my job was a proper daily routine, providing stability, which all of us dogs need to have in life. It was safe and comfy in the office and my colleagues were lovely. I vowed never to seek adventure during office hours again!

Chapter 16

MEETING THE KENT PACK

The next weekend promised to be very exciting, because on the Sunday, I was going to a party in Kent and I would be meeting most of my extended pack members (Mum's family). On the downside, it was a long way away and that meant going in the car. If I didn't manage to hold on to my breakfast, I would have to lay in it for a long time before we could stop the car and it would be yet another embarrassing 'first impression gone wrong' for me.

On the Sunday morning, Mum took the precaution of just giving me a biscuit, with the promise of a full breakfast on arrival in Kent. I was very excited to be going to a party, especially as it was a 'little people's' party. I was thrilled to bits to learn that I had cute little people in my extended pack. I couldn't wait to meet them all.

I learnt that all the time the car was on the big Motorway roads I didn't feel sick at all. It was only the windy roads that churned up my tummy. So, I arrived at 'Aunty Carol and Uncle Rob's' house, breakfast and carrot free and full of anticipation at meeting everyone.

Mum and Dad took me in and as everyone made a huge, welcoming fuss of me, the tail did the full cycle, snake and all. For some reason, everyone,
especially the cute little people, thought that this was very funny and for the first time, I began to realise

that maybe it wasn't something to be so embarrassed about. If it made people happy, especially little people, then it can't be such a bad thing, can it?

I was made very welcome and some pack members had even bought me a little welcoming gift, which I thought was really sweet and thoughtful. Of course they got an extra big thank you slobber in return.

I had my breakfast as promised then went out to play in Aunty Carol and Uncle Rob's big garden with the little people. That was great fun and second only to hoovering up leftovers that I had found on paper plates.

I was the new pack member and consequently the main talking point. I was thoroughly enjoying all the attention and did what should be done at any party… I mingled and graciously accepted as much fuss and compliments as one dog could possibly handle in one day.

This was an awfully big pack and I was introduced to everyone, but I knew that it would take me a few parties to remember all their names. I needn't have worried though, because we visit our Kent pack quite often, so it didn't take me long to get to know them all properly.

Some of Mum and Dad's friends would regularly come up to visit us too, which saved me that dreaded car trip. Aunty Dorothy and her friend and Aunty Pauline, Uncle Andrew and Hayden would often come for a visit and it was always lovely to see them.

There were others of my own kind in the extended pack too….

There's Poppy, the little Dachshund, who is quite elderly and has diabetes and is sadly blind, but she still loves life and manages to have fun. She owns Nanny and Grandad.

There's Mica and Macey, who own Aunty Debs, Uncle Dan and their little people, Joseph and Katie.

Mica is a tiny Pom x and as you know, I have in the past, had some unhappy experiences with tiny dogs, but Mica is really cool. He's a big dog in little dog's clothing and we are good buddies.

Macey is a true hound dog. She is a Beagle x and has a really impressive hound dog bark, which sort of tails off into a howl. She's cool too and is even worse than me for stealing food. Respect!

There's Jasper, who owns Uncle Mark and Aunty Sonia and their little people, Brandon and Liberty. He is an elderly Lab, but although he adores little people, he isn't as keen on his fellow canines, so I have never actually met him 'in the fur'. He's not too keen on noisy parties either so he always stays at home.

Dad's sister, my Aunty Louise, has a very elderly terrier called Mille, who is very cantankerous and loves her Mum Louise, but hates everyone else.

There are often parties to attend in Kent and occasionally, despite only having one small biscuit prior to setting off in the car, I have a mishap on the way down and have to be cleaned up before I can join in the fun. Despite this, they all still love me and always make me welcome.

Anyway, going back to my first party……

There was music and games and little people running around playing chase, but bestest of all there was food and lots of it! My instincts were telling me to sneak and scoff down everything in sight, but Mum was keeping a very close eye on me, especially around the little people. My drool ducts were in overdrive and the temptation was overwhelming, but every time I almost got my gnashers locked onto the crust of a curled up sandwich being held in the hands of one of the little people, Mum was there like a shot.

I suppose looking back; it was a good thing she was really, as I probably wouldn't have been at all popular if I had stolen food from the little people on my first meeting with everyone.

I was keen to make a good first impression and be on my bestest behaviour.

The party was in full swing. The big people were all gathered in the kitchen. Uncle Steve was telling rude jokes, his sons, Sam and Stuart, were talking about motorbikes and the little people were all rampaging around outside in the garden making an impressively deafening amount of noise. I was joining in with the rampaging and having a thoroughly great time, when all of a sudden, I felt a sharp pain in my tummy.

The sausage rolls, cakes and sweeties that I had manage to steal unnoticed from the table, along with the paper plates they were on, had all got thoroughly churned up in my tummy and needed to be evacuated very urgently.

I gave Mum the slip and frantically looked for a suitably discreet place to relieve myself and decided that behind the huge oak tree at the bottom of the garden would be the perfect spot. Nobody would notice me behind there.

I trotted off as nonchalantly as possible and dived behind the massive tree trunk out of view.

Once I was sure that I hadn't been noticed, I quickly deposited my unwanted load and I have to admit that even by my standards it was really quite huge and disgusting.

I had concealed it behind a big tree and nobody saw me do it, so I was feeling very pleased with myself for being so discreet and thoughtful and was feeling lots better without that awful pain in my tummy.

I was definitely a fair bit lighter too. Yay! Loads of room for more party food!

I made my way back to my new little playmates and carried on playing as though nothing had happened.

After a while, my little pals decided that they wanted to play racing games on the battery jeeps that were kept in the summerhouse.

As there was no room in the jeeps for a large hound, I had to take a rain check and sit and watch while they charged around in them and argued over who was going in which jeep and who was driving etc. etc. I didn't mind at all and was enjoying the rest to be honest.

All was fine until I noticed that the boy's jeep was fast heading towards the big oak tree where I had offloaded earlier. I watched nervously as they got nearer and nearer to it, and as the jeep disappeared behind it, I realised what was about to happen and ran for cover.

The jeep re-appeared from behind the tree and came zooming back up the garden at full speed and suddenly, it was like the parting of the waves.

Mum's were grabbing their little people and running towards the house screaming as the jeep wheels span round, flinging sloppy dollops of my discarded bowel contents, high and wide, pebble-dashing everyone and everything within a 15 foot radius.

Aunty Carol was shrieking at the boys to "STOP!" as everyone scattered in all directions to avoid being spattered.

Eventually, the boys heard her shouting above the screams and came to a stop in the middle of the lawn, wondering what on earth all the fuss was about. They thought that it was hilarious, everyone running round like mad things.

Once the jeep was finally stationary, the driver and passengers were lifted out, sniffed and carefully inspected for brown spots.

Being inside the jeep, they had luckily escaped any direct hits, but the few people that hadn't run fast enough unfortunately hadn't been so lucky and had to borrow clothing from Aunty Carol's wardrobes.

Poor Mum was cringing with embarrassment as she slunk out to the garden, red-faced, with a bucket of disinfectant and an old brush to rid the jeep tyres of what was left of my smelly deposit.

She was out there for ages scrubbing the deeply grooved plastic tyres and scouring the huge lawn for any remnants that had not attached themselves to moving targets.

Of course, being 'just a dog', I was not blamed at all and was even praised for my thoughtfulness in trying to do my biz as far away from the little people as possible.

Obviously it was totally the owners responsibility to watch their dog and clean up after him, so while the guilty party was outside doing what she had failed to do in the first place, I, of course was indoors playing with my new little friends and making the most of the guilty party not being there to watch me like a hawk.

As I gently slid another yummy ham sandwich from between sticky little fingers and swallowed it whole, I thought to myself that this was certainly a memorable party.

All too soon it was time to head home. Little people were getting irritable and needed their beds and I too was very tired and full of stolen sandwiches.

I felt that it was my duty to eat as much as I could get my teeth into as everyone had been commenting on how terribly skinny I was, but also how adorable and friendly I was too. I just hoped that I was able to hold on to my ill-gotten gains on the way home in the car.

All in all, it was a very good day and despite the embarrassing jeep incident, I had earnt my place in the extended pack. I had charmed them all and had everyone tucked securely under my paw.

We said our goodbyes and got in the car.

I slept all the way home with a smile on my muzzle and was too tired to even think about carrots.

I had pleasant dreams of sausage rolls, cakes, happy, smiley faces and me chasing little squealing people, pinning them down and slobbering all over them.

It was such a lovely dream, that I was a tad miffed when Dad woke me up by opening the car door and telling me to get my furry butt out of the car and indoors.

I dutifully hopped out and went indoors, and curled up on my sofa. As I drifted back off to sleep, I wondered when my next exciting party would be.

Chapter 17

REDUNDANT

I had been living with Mum and Dad for several weeks now and had got used to the routines of daily life. With the aid of a trip to see a nice lady vet, who gave me some medicine, my tummy was finally beginning to settle down. The vet explained to Mum that we Lurchers are very 'sensitive little souls' and are easily upset by changes.

She assured her that my tummy would settle in time. Of course she was spot on. I had to deal with a lot of changes within a few months and although the latter ones were all good changes (except for the theft of my assets of course!), it was still an awful lot for a 'sensitive little soul' to cope with.

To help with my delicate tummy problem on a more permanent basis, Mum had also changed my food to this 'hypo-something or other' food stuff, which I was quite happy about as it was very tasty!

I was just starting to feel settled and had a nice routine going, when one day at work, there was a big kerfuffle developing in the meeting room. I got up and wandered in to try and find out what was going on. I kept hearing the strange words 'redundancy' and 'redundant' cropping up in the banter and Dad and the ladies seemed far from happy. In fact, I was picking up on a lot of negative energy here.

Something was very wrong.

After much uncomfortable straining of ears and lots of concentration trying to piece together all of the words that I knew in order to find out what was occurring. I found out that the office would be closing down and that soon, Dad and I wouldn't be allowed to come to work anymore.

I was ecstatically happy at the thought of retiring so young, but very sad to think that I wouldn't see my ladies every day.

I would also miss the burger van and the little people's club up the road, but it would be nice to stay at home with Dad, even if it was only until we got another job.

Maybe it wouldn't be so bad after all.

We carried on going in to work, until one day, the last day had arrived. We had a little farewell bash in the meeting room and that was to be the last time that I set paw in my office.

It was a very sad day indeed, but it was made much more bearable by the presentation of my leaving gift, a yummy piece of fried chicken from the red and white smiley man's shop, just for me.

We said our farewells, shook paws and hugged and we all went home from work for the last time.

I still to this day occasionally see my ladies and get to give them a slobber for old time's sake.

We are still all good friends and always will be.

Chapter 18

LIFE ON THE DOLE

After getting used to being a 9-5 office hound, it felt very strange, but also very nice being at home all day with Dad.

He spent a lot of time on his computer looking for a new job for us to go to every day and a big part of the day on his x-box thingy, which was ok because I got to lay down on the sofa with him.

For some of the day, we played together with my toys. This was my favourite part of being 'on the dole'.

Every day, just before Mum was due to come home, Dad would jump up and rush around pretending to get on with those boring old household chores. He made me promise not to tell her about this.

I agreed after a bribe of a pig's ear.

I will fess up and admit that in the early days, I got very stressed if Mum and Dad both went out and left me in the house on my own.

The first time they did it, I got worried about them and went down the wooden hill and tried to dig my way through the carpet and wall and into the front room where the birds lived, so I could go and look for them. There were no doors to separate the rooms downstairs then, so I wasn't allowed to roam around on my own near the birds in case I got tempted to try and play with them.

Because of this little incident, on the days that Dad had to put his 'posh pelt' on and go out to see a man about a job, or to go to the jobcentre place, I went to work with Mum.

It was ok, because Mum was able to move her desk down the wooden hill so that I could go out in the garden when I needed to and even sunbathe on nice days, though she would keep calling me in to cool off every now and then.

I am an avid sun-worshipper and given the chance, will lay stretched out in the midday sun until I am slow roasted to medium-rare or even well done.

It was a bit boring on cold or wet days, but hey, at least I wasn't home alone.

I had my duvet and toys and on very cold days, I would whine louder and louder until Mum took the hint and came over to cover me up and tuck me in.

I eventually got the office guys trained to do this as well, so if Mum had to pop out, they would take it in turns to come down and cover me up.

I remember one freezing day at work, Mum had disappeared up the wooden hill and I was cold and desperately needed covering up, so I started to whine.

When this failed to bring her running, I escalated to full blown howling and singing so that she would hear.

When she came down, she was a bit cross with me because they were having some sort of phone conference meeting thing with a client and everyone could hear me singing. Fancy that, I had taken part in my first conference call meeting!

I wondered what sort of new job I would be going to with Dad. I was happy enough at home with him, or working the odd day with Mum and I felt guilty for not being happy with my lot, but I was so hoping he would line up something a bit more exciting for us than office work next time.

Maybe we would be driving high-speed trains, or speedboats, or maybe I would be Dad's Co-Pilot in a super-Sonic jet! yay! My namesake!

Yes, I do watch Bond films with Dad, how did you guess?

Dad shattered all my fantasies about being a Hot Shot career hound when he took me to one side and explained that once he had found a new job, I would be going to work with Mum every day.

He said that wherever he would end up, it would almost certainly not be 'dog friendly' like our last place of work.

Oh well, no exciting career prospects for me then. There would be no more burger vans or little people's clubs either. Still, I had got used to Mum's office and although the guys didn't fuss over me like my ladies did at my old company, I liked them and once they got used to me, they seemed to like me too.

Dad did find a new job and as he had said would probably be the case, it seems that I was not welcome there, so I would have to go to work with Mum every day once Dad started his new job.

It wasn't as much fun, but at least I would be with Mum all day.

Life was still good.

Chapter 19

THE PHOTO SHOOT

One morning, Mum spotted an advert in the local paper for a Doggie Photo Competition being held at our local pet store.

Apparently, the winner from each region would then be entered into a National Competition.

Mum was very excited about this and said that as I was so handsome, I would be in with a chance and that it would be lovely to have some decent photos of me taken by a professional.

So it looked like I was going to have to practice my cheesy grin and posing techniques.

On the morning of the competition, I was subjected to an awful bathing session and upon drying, was mortified to see that I had ended up with the most enormous, fluffy, uncontrollable twizzle I had ever had in my life.

To add insult to injury, the old knickers were extra fluffy and were flapping around in the breeze much more than was acceptable for a big macho hound like me.

I was most unimpressed, but Mum was very pleased with my appearance and even tried to blow dry and backcomb my fluffy bits to add even more volume, but I was having none of that, I was off like a shot!

Dad, bless him, was as disgusted as me and bravely launched an undercover mission to try to prevent certain ridicule, by snipping off the embarrassing twizzle and knickers to preserve my dignity–and his, but he was thwarted. Despite deploying military standard stealth tactics, he was detected, intercepted and defeated by Mum just as the scissors were being wielded.

And so off I trotted to the pet store, twizzle and knickers in all their brilliant white, mega fluffy glory, streaming out behind me in the breeze. I was so embarrassed.

When I got there, I realised that I needn't have worried, because there were some poor souls that had obviously been subjected to many hours of fluffing and titivating and were in a much worse state than me. At least all my embarrassing bits were confined to my back end and I can sit on them to hide them, but some of these poor things were just head to tail fluffballs!

There were an awful lot of purebreds queuing up to see the photographer, all looking very posh and regal and were obviously very proud to be representing their breed. I began to wonder if this might be one of Mum's many 'not so good' ideas, but then I was very relieved to see a few crossbreeds like myself joining the long queue. There were even some very elderly, but still very handsome Golden Oldies. I felt a bit better and decided to relax and just try to enjoy the experience.

As we got nearer to the front of the queue, I noticed lots of 'sample' photos dotted around the table and on the walls. This guy was good! Some of the dogs in the photos were obviously not the best looking hounds you would meet, but he had managed to capture all of their best qualities and had made them all look very handsome indeed.

I was wondering what my photos would be like. Maybe he could somehow make the old scars on my head disappear and make the big bony lump over my eye socket look flatter.

Although I was still very handsome, these permanent reminders of my traumatic past were quite noticeable.

Eventually it was my turn and the man said "next please". I eagerly rushed over to introduce myself, dragging Mum behind, who had linked arms with Dad, so he came horizontally at great speed too.

As we all arrived in front of the photographer in an undignified rabble, he asked us to fill in a form and then I had to go over and stand on this very posh podium that had fake grass, a fence and plastic leaves and flowers.

As I was a bit nervous, my bladder was twitching and I seriously contemplated lifting my leg at the gate post, but then remembered the 'no peeing indoors' rule, so decided I had better hold onto it.

The photographer man asked Mum if I knew how to sit on command. Blooming cheek! I wasn't a puppy and it was one of the first things Mum had taught me, after the no peeing indoors rule.

I sat down, nose in the air to show my disgust at his insulting remark, (and also to show off my best side) and Mum backed away.

I sat there for a few seconds while the man was fiddling about with his black photo box and I started to get bored, so while he was messing around, I jumped off and went to check out the rawhide chews in the next aisle. I knew where everything was in here. It was my favourite shop!

Dad chased after me and hauled me back over to the podium. I was told to sit again, and so I sat. Again the man was fiddling about and I was getting very bored with the whole thing. I concluded that being a model was not the most exciting job in the world and wondered how full time models ever managed to even stay awake.

I was suddenly distracted by a rather gorgeous looking young red setter girl about halfway down the aisle near the cat food and trotted off to chat her up.

Dad headed me off and grabbed my collar. On the way back to the boring podium, he told me I was being very naughty and that I had to sit still, so I did. He said "NO, not here you donut, over there!" Humans can be so confusing! I was then dragged back over to the podium and told to sit down and STAY!

Once again, the photographer had to fiddle about with his black box and I was just about to jump off and go over and ask the girls on the till for a treat to chew on while I was waiting (they always keep a bowl of treats at the till and I always get at least one just before we leave the store), when Mum called me.

I looked over at her and noticed that she was waving something around, right next to the photographer's right ear. I was intrigued and tried to focus on this thing being waved in the air. It looked familiar. Mum stopped waving it around and held it still for a second. I zoomed in on it and then realisation dawned. Joy of all joys, It was a treat!

My eyes expanded to saucer like proportions, my radars pricked up, the initial stages of the drooling process had kicked in and in that split second before I leapt off of the boring podium and thundered over to collect my treat, there was a big white flash, which temporarily blinded me and a little cheer went up from the audience that I had inadvertently drawn in to watch this amusing little show.

The photographer, who had started to develop a twitch around his eyes and mouth and had begun tugging at his hair for some reason, seemed recharged with enthusiasm at his little triumph and stated that he wanted another shot of me sitting and then one of me laying down. "If he knows how to do that", he added. I was so not amused by this remark. I was a Lurcher. Lying down is what I did best for goodness sake!

After several more kerfuffles and much twitching and hair tugging later, the photographer triumphantly declared that he had finished and that he had actually managed to get some very good shots-under the circumstances.

He gradually stopped the twitching and hair tugging and gave me yet another biscuit and said goodbye.

He was a very nice man after all.

I collected my treats from the till girls on my way out and decided that all in all, the photo shoot had been a good experience.

Mum and Dad were trembling and twitching a bit, which I thought was odd, as it was certainly not a cold day. I was concerned that they might be coming down with something, maybe the same twitchy virus as the Photographer man had. They said that they desperately needed a cup of hot, sweet tea for their nerves and a lie down in a darkened room.

A week later, we had to go back to the pet store to view my photos and select which one we wanted to enter into the competition. We could also decide if we wanted to buy any of them to take home and keep.

When we saw them, we were all gob smacked.

As you know, I am quite a handsome chap anyway, but these photos made me look like a film star. No, really, they did. This guy was a genius! You couldn't see the scars and the lump on my head at all and this clever man had captured my intense, 'focussed on the treat' look perfectly.

Ok, if you wanted to be very picky and pedantic, you might point out that my eyes looked to be in real danger of falling out of their sockets and there was the tiniest hint of drool at the corners of my mouth (well they were my favourite treats!), but your average person would never notice and probably just say that I looked very alert and intelligent.

Dad selected the one of me sitting to be entered into the competition, but Mum pointed out that due to my very short fur underneath, my boy's bits and pieces were on display for all to see. Of course, being male and proud of it, I couldn't see what her problem was and neither could Dad (we always back each other up on the guys stuff), but she said it might put the judges off (blooming cheek of her!) and so it was decided that the 'head and shoulders' shot would be a much more appropriate one to be scrutinised by the judges, especially if they were ladies.

Mum and Dad bought 3 of my photos, including the one in the front of this book, which is the one that was entered into the competition. Of course Mum and Dad wanted to buy all of them, but we just chose the best 3. They were all really great photos and worth every penny as far as I am concerned. I think Mum and Dad had to agree.

Several weeks later, we got a letter saying that I had won third place in the Regional Competition! Mum and Dad were chuffed to bits, and I was over the moon.

Best of all, I got a £10.00 gift voucher to spend in the pet store on whatever I wanted. Mum was so proud of me that she actually had a little tear or two, ahh bless.

We raced up to the store to spend my voucher. There was so much stuff there I wanted, that it took me ages to choose. I think we were in there for well over an hour.

In the end, I selected a tug ball, some diet ears (dried cow ears), a squeaky toy and a big beef knuckle bone. I chose them all myself and picked them off of the shelves and gave them to Mum to put in the trolley. It actually came to over £13.00, but hey, I've never been much into maths. Mum said she didn't mind and was so proud of me that she would pay the extra. Funny, I just knew she would say that.

I spent a lovely afternoon enjoying my prizes and as we all went up to bed that night, Mum gave me an extra big hug and fuss and said "That wasn't a bad result for an ex-Battersea street hound was it Sonic".

Despite my exuberant and sometimes downright destructive behaviour, Mum always says that my previous family must have been completely bonkers and stupid to abandon me and that it was their loss and her gain, and Dad's of course and do you know, I reckon she is right.

Chapter 20

DEW CLAWS…..WHY?!

I once heard that people are born with something inside them called an appendix, which is of no use or value to their lives whatsoever. In fact, sometimes, these things can go horribly wrong and cause all sorts of dreadful pain and problems.

We canines have exactly the same issue with dew claws…..

The very fortunate few are lucky enough to be born without them and some have them taken off by a vet soon after being born, but the rest of us have to suffer the consequences of these useless, dangly digits, dangerously flapping around our legs.

I suppose I should consider myself slightly more fortunate than some, in that I only have them on my front legs. Some poor souls are blighted with 4 of the things, one on each leg. Some very, very unlucky individuals actually have multiple ones on each leg. How unlucky is that?!

You do sort of get used to them just being there and even forget that you have them, but sometimes, something happens that gives you a very painful reminder of their existence!................

It was September and a gloriously sunny, Saturday lunchtime and my day was going well. I had popped in to the R.S.P.C.A charity shop at the end of our road with Mum, to say hello to the lovely ladies and the nice man that manage it and after getting back home, I had a little rest on the sofa before going outside to play in the sunshine.

I was happily charging around, chasing flies and playing with my toys, when I suddenly slipped and lost all control over my legs for a split second (easily done when you have gangly limbs like mine). I sort of tilted over to one side and skidded along the ground, legs flailing around all over the place and suddenly, there was this excruciating pain in my left front leg. Although I am normally a very brave chap (for a Lurcher), the pain was so intense that I emitted the loudest, longest, howly scream I have ever produced in my life.

Mum and Dad came charging out with sheer panic on their faces and saw me holding up my horribly injured leg, trembling with fright and pain.

Mum rushed over and hugged me and then she gently took my leg to assess the damage. I had been much too afraid to look myself, given the level of agony I was suffering, I was sure that my whole leg must be hanging off or something.

She sighed with relief and told Dad that it was ok, as I had ONLY broken my dew claw. If I wasn't in so much pain, I might have swatted her with my twizzle for that cutting, off-hand remark.

She then said that it was snapped right at the top and would be very painful (no kidding!), so she couldn't just snip it off herself, without me screaming the neighbourhood down and the RSPCA knocking on the door soon afterwards.

There was nothing for it. I had to go to the vet.

Mum rang a local vet and they said that they had literally only just closed their routine surgery a few minutes earlier and I was therefore now classed as an out of hours emergency.

I thought this sounded very dramatic and it made me feel very important.

I was hoping that Mum would stick a little blue light on top of her car and get it to make those siren noises that I have heard emergency vehicles make.

I was lifted into the car and off we went. I waited with baited breath but there were no blue light or siren noises. I couldn't help feeling a little cheated to be honest.

I overheard Mum and Dad saying that it was so annoying that I hadn't busted my claw 10 minutes earlier during normal surgery hours. Oh, wasn't that just charming don't you think?! There was I, laying there in absolute agony, bleeding to death (well, bleeding anyway) and they were just moaning about having to pay three times as much for my treatment. How mean were they. I was worth it!

We got to the vets quite quickly and Dad lifted me out. I hobbled painfully in to the surgery and this large man vet came out and asked us to 'go through'. He looked at my horrific injury and said that there were two options. 1.(the cheapest option) was that he could just 'snip it off', but that would hurt. It would hurt a lot; but, he stressed, only for a split second.

Or option 2.(the much more expensive option) was to knock me out to do it, so I wouldn't feel it at all. Mum said that she could have snipped it off herself but didn't want me to suffer that kind of pain, even for a split second, so they agreed on Option 2, to knock me out.

I was nervously wondering what would hurt more, having the claw snipped off, or being hit on the head, when I was relieved to discover that knocking me out meant just a small injection to make me sleep and not being hit on the head until I was unconscious.

I was so pleased that Mum and Dad went for option 2. They were lovely and not mean after all.

The nice big man vet trimmed the fur on my leg for some reason (I was in too much pain to question why he was shaving my legs) and Mum gave me a nice hug.

I was very brave with needles and didn't mind at all when he put the needle in my leg. In fact, I was just in the process of trying to give him a snuffle and slobber in his left earhole, when the room started spinning, my legs started to crumple and suddenly, everything went black.

The next thing I remember was waking up, seeing Mum and Dad sitting on the floor with me, looking all concerned yet relieved at the same time. I could see their blurry faces, all 8 of them, swirling around and zooming in and out and I could hear their voices, but it sounded like they were speaking in slow motion, whilst eating, in a tunnel, under water.

As my eyes and ears gradually adjusted back to normal, I was aware that the sharp pain had gone from my leg and there was a dull throb instead. I anxiously glanced down and was relieved to see that my leg was still present, but it had a humungous great green bandage on it. I would soon get that off!

I eventually managed to scrabble to my feet, but it was touch and go for a while. I was a bit like a new born baby giraffe (I watch all the nature programmes on the TV box).

Mum and Dad supported me until I was less baby giraffe-like and could walk unaided, except for a minor blip where I somehow fell over my bandage.

Mum and Dad paid at the desk and off we went home, where I slept very soundly for the next several hours. I must say that it was the best sleep I have ever had. No dreaming, no waking up at every little sound, nothing. Just peaceful, black nothingness.

Once I had woken up a bit more and had staggered to the garden for a wee and then had some dinner, I set about the task of removing the bandage. I had just got my teeth into the first bit and was tugging furiously, when Mum appeared out of nowhere and advanced at great speed, brandishing that rotten plastic funnel and promptly rammed it over my head.

I thought I had seen the last of that evil thing when my stitches were removed, but obviously she had sneakily tucked it away for future torturing sessions!

At that point I decided to give up and I went back to sleep, though this time, I did wake up at the slightest noise and I had a really horrible dream about being suffocated by a big plastic bucket and having all my toenails snipped off right at the top, one by one, without the knocking out stuff.

Boy was I glad that they went for option 2.

Chapter 21

MEETING THE SEASIDE PACK

I have two Nannies and two Grandads.
One Nanny and Grandad, who you already know, live in Kent.
The other Nanny and Grandad live by the seaside in Hampshire.
I will tell you about the day I first met my seaside Nanny and Grandad……..

It was a weekend and Mum and Dad announced that we were going to see Nanny and Grandad. Naturally I assumed that we were off to Kent for the day and got very excited. I loved going to see the Kent pack. I always got loads of attention all day.
As we drove off, I settled myself on my duvet in the back and drifted off to sleep.
Before I knew it, the car had stopped and Mum and Dad were opening the doors and getting out. I sat up all bleary eyed and had a big yawn.
What the……..where the hell were we?!………………
There was this huge great river with brown banks and these enormous white birds swooping around making a right old racket. They were even more gobby than Jack parrot.
I sniffed the air and it had this weird salty tang to it. What on earth had happened to Kent?

Dad opened the back of the car and I cautiously hopped out. Those huge white squawking featherbags were terrifying!

Mum and Dad told me that this place was called 'the seaside'.

The big river they call the Thames, is really big, but I had never seen anything like this in London and the water was moving and coming towards us. It was very scary indeed.

As I padded along on the strange dusty riverbank with Mum and Dad, I started to relax and enjoy the wonderful new sniffs. There were pieces of smelly, crunchy, dead little animals on the ground and I managed to grab one and eat it before Mum could stop me. It was really salty and delicious and I discreetly looked for more.

After we had been walking for a little while, Mum and Dad turned and walked towards the moving water. I was fascinated by it. When the water first rushed towards my paws, I shot backwards and almost pulled my head out of my collar, but once I realised that it wasn't going to hurt, I carefully dipped a paw in. OMG! It was freezing! But it was fun, so I decided to put all 4 paws in and see how it felt. It was nice actually, once the freezing feeling had worn off a bit, it sort of tickled as the water moved back and forth over my paws. I knew what it smelt like, but I decided to see what this new, exciting water tasted like so I took a big mouthful and after managing not to lose my breakfast in the car, I almost brought it up.

It was vile tasting water, yucky, yuk! I knew not to ever do that again.

After a while, Mum and Dad said that we would go round to see Nanny and Grandad and we went back to the car.

I assumed that Nanny and Grandad had moved from their usual home in Kent, to a new one at this seaside place, so I got in the car and curled up to lick my salty, gritty and smelly, but strangely pleasantly tasting paws.

I had only managed to get one paw reasonably clean and presentable when Dad announced that we were there. Wow! Nanny and Grandad lived very near the big salty river.

As we walked up the path to the new house, the door opened and I was about to greet Nan, when I was confronted by a lady that was not Nanny. Mum said that this was Nanny, but it sure as hell wasn't. She was nice though and so was the man that Mum said was Grandad, though he clearly wasn't Grandad. What on earth was going on?

I could smell a cat! She was apparently shut in one of the bedrooms so that I couldn't chase her. Pah, spoilsports!

Suddenly, this small to medium sized crossbreed appeared, right in my face. I really do mean right in my face. He charged at me at full speed and demanded that I play. I am usually very polite, but I wasn't having this whippersnapper disrespect me like that so I growled at him to back off.

His name was Blackie and actually, once he had backed off a bit, I decided that he was ok. He also had loads of bowls of biscuits and toys dotted around, so we would get on just fine thank you very much!

After Blackie had shown me around his garden and house and told me all about the locals, we laid down on the floor and listened to the banter between the pack.

I slowly pieced words together and realised that this was indeed my Nanny and Grandad. They were Dad's Mum and Dad. What a relief! I hadn't lost my other nice Nan and Grandad at all. They were Mum's Mum and Dad and were still there in Kent. I had just gained another nice Nanny and Grandad to visit. Result!

I had just drifted off into a nice little sleep, when the doorbell rang and woke me up. A man and a little person came in. I immediately tried to lovingly pin the little person down and administer the ritual slobbery greetings, but he seemed terrified of me and started to cry. I must admit to feeling a little hurt and dejected by his reaction. I only wanted to be nice to him.

Mum explained that he was only small and I was huge and must have scared him. His name was Josh and he was scared of all dogs except Blackie.

I felt a bit better knowing it was nothing personal and decided that I would do my best to convince him that most other dogs are really nice too. Especially me!

The man was cool. He was Dad's brother Iain and I really liked him because he said I had big muscles! I decided he would make a very good seaside Uncle.

There was another treat in store for me, because my Seaside Nanny and Grandad looked after a great little place that backed onto their garden, which they called 'The Secret Garden' and Blackie and I were let loose in it to run around like crazy hounds. Blackie did get a bit scared a few times as I came charging out of the undergrowth towards him at top speed, but he was up for a game.

We had a lovely time in there, playing 'chase me'. I did slow down to let him catch me once or twice otherwise he might have got bored and gone home. I was crashing through the pathways, when I saw a patch of bright green grass over to my right. I ran over to it at top speed and as my front paws hit the bright green patch, they fell away from me and I ended up submerged head first in black, smelly pond water. Well, it did look like grass, honestly it did!

After an emergency clean up and some tea, we said our goodbyes to the seaside pack and headed off home.

It had been an exhausting but very exciting day. I now had two Nannies and Grandad's to look forward to visiting.

As I dozed off in the back of the car, I smiled to myself and thought how wonderful my new life was.

And so was that smelly, crunchy, dead little thing that I had found near that big salty river.

Chapter 22

MY FIRST PROPER CHRISTMAS

I had been living at home for 7 months and was well and truly settled into the routines of daily pack life with Mum and Dad, and was now looking forward to my very first 'proper' Christmas. I had heard a lot about this special day called Christmas.

It was a time for eating as much as you could, then being sick and starting all over again. Sounded like great fun to me! I also heard that if you were good all year, a nice, big, bearded man in a red velvet suit and hat would give you presents of toys and food.

I thought back over the year and was certain that I hadn't done anything bad enough to jeopardise my chances of landing a prezzie or two, but Mum said that there was still time, so I had to be on my bestest behaviour if I wanted any presents from the big man called Santa.

One day, as the big day drew nearer, Dad suddenly clambered up some strange portable metal stairs and disappeared into the ceiling. I was intrigued and desperately wanted to follow him to investigate, but my paws wouldn't grip the stairs and I slipped and banged my chin, so I had to sit and wait, peering anxiously up at the black hole.

I could hear rustling noises and the occasional thud, followed by 'naughty Dad words'. I assumed that he was probably banging his head or toe up there.

At last, Dad appeared in the black hole, carrying a long box with a photo of a tree on it. He slowly came down backwards and trod on my nose and almost fell off of the metal stairs when I screeched in pain and surprise. Humans are just so clumsy!

Dad said sorry, but told me I shouldn't have been so nosey, then he laid the box in the bedroom and off he went up in the ceiling again. I performed a cursory sniff along the box, but was unable to determine the nature of its contents. It wasn't food that's for sure, so I soon lost interest.

Dad came back down carrying a smaller, square box with sparkly bits hanging out of the top. I quickly backed up to remove my already throbbing nose out of the way of his big feet, and then rushed over to sniff the new box as soon as it was safe to do so. Again there were no food aromas, so I went down the wooden hill to watch the TV box.

Eventually, Dad came down with the boxes and opened them up on the floor. I went over to see what was inside. There was nothing interesting on the TV box anyway. I was puzzled to see bits of a folded up plastic tree in one, and tubs of balls and sparkly things in the other. I cautiously sniffed each item as it emerged from the boxes, and could not work out what was going on, so I decided to recline on the sofa and just see what Dad was going to do with all this weird stuff.

I watched in wonder as Dad made a big tree out of the bits in the long box. I wondered if I would be allowed to pee up it, then decided that it would probably be a NO as it was a tree INSIDE the house. See, I do figure things out for myself!

Once he had finished making the big plastic tree, he walked round and round it, putting a long twisty rope around the branches. He then went to the other box and pulled out some sparkly rope, which he also draped around the tree.

Next he got some small, shiny balls and other little dangly thingy's out of the boxes and hung them on the tree branches with bits of string. I was totally flummoxed as to what this was all about, but it was slightly more entertaining than watching football on the TV box anyway.

Just as I was about to nod off, he pushed the end of the twisty rope into the wall and flicked a switch.

I almost fell off the sofa in shock and surprise as the tree suddenly lit up like a… well….like a Christmas tree! I realised there and then why people use that saying. It was the first Christmas tree I had ever seen, and it was well and truly lit up!

After I had recovered from the initial shock, I stretched out along the sofa and just stared at it for the longest time. It was the most beautiful thing I had ever seen (apart from when I first saw Speck of course, but I'll tell you all about that wonderful day a bit later on).

I was fascinated with the lights twinkling in the branches and once the novelty had started to wear off a bit, I thought it might be fun to play with the balls that were dangling from the ends of the branches, but first I would check them out for gaming suitability.

Dad had gone back up into the ceiling with the empty boxes, so I decided to test the balls for bounce, durability and fetchability.

As I gently teased the first one off of its branch, it slipped and fell onto the floor. Yay! It bounced! I spent a few minutes batting it around the floor and decided to bite it to test for durability. There was a loud popping noise that hurt my ears and made me jump, and the ball sort of crumpled up into a little heap. Ew, cheap and nasty!

I decided to choose another. The same thing happened and another and another.

Suddenly there was a loud "NOOOO!" as Mum appeared, along with Dad, who was back from putting the empty boxes in the ceiling, and they had both bellowed at me in unison.

They didn't seem too pleased with me regarding the ball durability testing, and there was even mention of telling Santa I had been very bad and therefore should be struck off of the present list.

I was very upset. After all, I was only trying to help. There's just no pleasing some people!

During the last few days running up to the big day, Mum was constantly sitting at the table, wrapping clothes, little people's toys and all sorts of other things in colourful paper and writing in cards and putting them into envelopes.

I didn't understand why she was doing it, because she obviously didn't want to. All the time, she kept making these big sighing noises and muttering under her breath about being glad it was only once a year and stuff like that.

Some of the wrapped up things were carefully stacked underneath the tree indoors, and Mum kept reminding me that if I touched the tree or anything on or under it, Santa would hear about it and might decide to leave me off of his 'presents for good woofies' list indefinitely!

Soon it was the night before the big day, and I was starting to get very excited.

Despite all Mum's threats of no presents from Santa, I knew for a fact that there was at least one squeaky toy with my name on it, because Mum had accidentally squeaked it during the wrapping process and then she immediately started to make coughing noises to try and disguise it.

One thing that humans should understand about squeaky toys, is that there is nothing on this planet that sounds quite like a squeaker, except a squeaker. They are unique, they are exciting, they just ARE!

Having said that, the evil Jack parrot can imitate a squeaker so accurately, that he regularly has me frantically running around the house in search of the new toy, until the penny drops, and I see him sitting on his perch looking smug and pleased with himself.

He even calls and whistles me using Mum or Dad's voice, the rotten featherbag. I swear I would pluck him if he wasn't so terrifying.

I galloped off up the hill to bed that night, full of anticipation and excitement. As I drifted off to sleep that Christmas Eve, I had visions of magical glowing squeakers in all different sizes, shapes and colours, along with huge, juicy bones, rolling out from under the Christmas tree and landing at my paws.

As I opened my bleary eyes early the next morning and the night fog in my brain began to clear, I was suddenly aware that it was Christmas Day!

The day of eating until you are sick and then starting all over again! The day of finding out once and for all if I had been a good enough hound all year to receive presents from the fat man in red! It was also the day of visiting the Kent pack!

I leapt up onto Mum and Dad's bed and jumped up and down, pretending that I desperately needed to go out for an emergency wee. Of course, I just wanted to go down the wooden hill to check under the tree to see if there was anything there for me.

Mum and Dad stirred, then sleepily mumbled happy Christmas to each other and me, made kissy noises and promptly snuggled down and tried to go back to sleep, but I wasn't having that! It was Christmas Day and it was my first 'proper' Christmas. I intended to enjoy every single minute of it and they had to get out of bed immediately!

I started fidgeting and when that didn't work, I started kicking my back legs out. No response, so I escalated my efforts to whining in Mum's ear. That worked a treat, and she sleepily crawled out of bed and put on her dressing gown.

I was down that hill in 2 bounds and under the tree before she even got to the landing. I had a quick ferret around under there and was mortified to find nothing that resembled a treat or a squeaky for me.

I was starting to panic. Maybe Santa really had been watching me when I had eaten that slime monster in the garden the other day without Mum and Dad seeing.

Maybe he had seen me sneakily tapping the tree balls with my paws and making them spin round, and maybe he even saw me craftily chewing the ones round the back without pulling them off.

So, they were not just idle threats to make me behave myself. Santa really was watching me and I had blown it.

I reversed out from under the tree, head bowed low, feeling very sorry for myself, and frankly a bit emotional, when Mum suddenly appeared in the doorway holding up a huge red sock stuffed with lumpy things.

I looked up and she smiled and said "Look Sonic, Santa's been and judging by all these presents with your name on them, you must have been a very good boy!" I couldn't believe my eyes and ears. I didn't even have to share presents with the birds, because Santa had left another big red sock full of presents for them too.

Dad came down and we all opened one present each. I eagerly ripped the paper off of mine and there it was, a blue, soft toy dog (rather like a caricature of myself actually), complete with extra loud squeaker!

While Mum and Dad gave the birds a present each and opened one themselves, I galloped around the

house in a hyper-hound state, with my very first Christmas squeaky clamped firmly between my teeth, squeaking for England! And the day had only just started! There would be more exciting stuff to come. After breakfast, we would be driving down to spend the rest of the day with the Kent pack, and when
we got back home, we could open the rest of our presents.

After Mum and Dad had taken paracetamol, the birds had unwrapped their presents, and we had finished breakfast (only one biscuit for me-just in case), me, Mum and Dad all got in the car and off we went to Kent.

When we pulled up outside Aunty Carol and Uncle Rob's house, Mum plonked an enormous pair of very embarrassing jingly antlers on my head and before I could protest, in we went.

I felt a right Charlie, jangling every time I moved my head, but the little people loved them, so it was ok I suppose.

I had a wonderful day with my lovely big pack, and I also got lots more prezzies.

I must admit to thinking that Santa must be getting a bit old and in need of stronger glasses. I wasn't a bad boy at all really, but there's no way I had been good enough to warrant all of those presents.

Still, I wasn't going to query it with the big fella. They were all mine and Dad would just have to make me a bigger toy box.

I had lots of treats as well as toys and even had some of the special Christmas turkey and beef dinner (a definite highlight of the day). Despite my
concerns, I was too tired on the way home in the car to even think about being sick; and I had actually eaten carrots for dinner!

All in all, it was one of the best days of my life, and the good news was that we get to do this every year! On the way home in the car, as I was sprawled out on my duvet in the dark, surrounded by my Christmas toys and gifts, I thought about my huge new packs, in Kent and Hampshire and felt all safe and warm inside knowing that they all loved me. I loved them back too, every single one of them.

As I drifted off into a contented sleep, I decided that as well as loving my new family to bits, I also loved Santa and I most definitely loved Christmas!

Chapter 23

NEW YEAR NEW PALS

After a nice Christmas and New Year break at home with Mum and Dad, it was soon time to go back to work.

I was now going to work with Mum every day and spent most of my working day under my duvet snoring loudly. Well it was January and none too warm in her office.

I had made a good friend in one of the guys who worked up the wooden hill. He said that he wanted to have a dog of his own one day, and he used to come down especially to say hello and play ball with me for a while.

The nice marketing man would come in and make a huge fuss of me too. Most times when he came, he would be wearing his 'posh pelt' and would have to spend ages removing my hair and drool from it before being able to visit clients.

Sometimes he would bring in another of my new canine friends called Pogo. Pogo is a whippet, and though I love him dearly, I just couldn't cope with him for more than an hour at a time.

I love to play and would tear around like a mad thing for several minutes, but then the Greyhound gene would kick in and I needed to be still and rest.

Pogo had no 'off button' and ran on rechargeable batteries.

I would tolerate him using my ribcage as a springboard for a little while and then I would have to get tough with him. The thing is, it didn't matter what I did or said, he would not take no for an answer.

Our meetings would always end up with me prostrate on the floor, twitching, gasping, and wheezing like an old man, with bloodshot eyes bulging out of their sockets. My blue tongue, resembling a rotten piece of old ham, would be draped across the floor and he would invariably tread on it whilst tearing around me in a big circle.

Occasionally he would do the wall of death and bounce off the walls instead of my ribs, just for a bit of variation.

Another good friend that used to come in to work to play with me was Pola. Pola was the boss's white German Shepherd, but Pola was definitely not my boss! He was just a huge pup, and like Pogo, he constantly wanted me to play.

He didn't bounce off my ribs like Pogo did, which was very lucky as he weighed twice as much as me and was still growing, but like Pogo, he would not take no for an answer.

Pola did have an off switch, but when I was gasping for air on the floor, he would still be far from flicking it. He would calmly lie down, watching me with interest, as my ham-like tongue flapped wildly up and down on the parquet. Then he would swat me in the eye with his huge polar bear paw.

He would also bark right in my face trying to make me get up, which was very unpleasant because he had the revolting habit of eating his own poo and could probably fell a fully grown bull elephant at 100 yards with that breath!

One of my other favourite new friends was the boss's young daughter. Not only was she a nice 'little person', she was one of Pola's pack members. She told me that when she was a big person, she was going to be a vet.

I love vets. They are clever people that know where we hurt and how to put us right again. She was great fun to play with too.

We would play tug o' war with my rope toy. I would hold one end with my teeth and she would hold the other end with hers. She was only small, so I used to let her win most times and pretend to fall over when she shook the rope. If her Dad had caught her with my slobbery old rope toy in her mouth, we both would have got told off, but he never caught us.

It was a new year, I had a new job and new workmates, and I was at last starting to feel settled again.

Chapter 24

REDUNDANT AGAIN

I just could not believe my ears………….

After getting used to my 2nd new job and making some great new friends, it was announced that Mum's office would be moving to a bigger place, which like Dad's new company, did NOT welcome office dog employees.

What was wrong with these companies? I was doing a sterling job ridding the garden of slime monsters and catching the office flies. Why were some people just not dog friendly?

I came to the only conclusion possible. The people running these companies must be 'cat people'!

There were lots of discussions at home about what would become of me once Mum's office had moved. Obviously, my radars were on high alert at all times. It was very worrying and very exhausting constantly straining my ears like that.

I soon overheard a conversation that made me feel lots better. I heard that whatever happened, I would stay with Mum and Dad, always and forever.

I heard Mum tell Dad that she would re-home him before me. She got a dirty look from Dad, but an extra big slobber from me for that!

Dad agreed that we would stick together as a pack no matter what happened. I relaxed a little after hearing that statement, but I was still concerned about exactly where I would be going and what I would be doing while Mum and Dad were at work all day.

I continued to go to work with Mum for several more weeks, but things were starting to change and I wasn't too happy about it.

Chapter 25

THE BIG BIRD HOUSE

One day, a really huge parcel arrived and I naturally assumed that it could be for me.

As I ran my quivering snout over the box, I failed to detect any traces of food, so went back to my sofa, satisfied that it wasn't for me after all.

I was very, very wrong!

Dad opened the box and pulled out a very large, flat, metal contraption. I watched with mild interest as he fussed around it, and then, all of a sudden, he tugged at the metal and the flat thing sprang up into a tall wire box. I didn't like the noise it made, but decided to be brave and go over to inspect it.

It was much like the houses that the birds lived in, but huge. I was wondering what this could mean, when I had a sudden thought which disturbed me a lot.

They were going to get another bird. An enormous bird!

I had recently overheard Mum telling Dad that it was much bigger and much cheaper than the largest one that they sell in the pet shop, and that she was glad that she had checked on ebay. I wondered at the time what she was on about. She must have been talking about the new bird. I hoped that it wasn't one of those emu birds that I had seen on the TV box recently.

They were huge and even scarier than Jack parrot.
What happened next threw me into a state of panic and confusion............

They put MY duvet and pillow, and MY toys inside it!

I couldn't believe the cheek of them. Did they honestly expect me to share my own bed and personal belongings with a smelly emu?
They left my stuff in it and nonchalantly went off to watch the TV box.
I stood there glaring at them, but they just ignored me. Confused and upset, I paced around wondering where the hell I was supposed to sleep.
Aha! They had forgotten to close the door, so I decided that until this rotten emu arrived, I would claim back my duvet and toys, and claim its brand new wire house into the bargain. That would show it its place in the pack!
As I sprawled out on my duvet, Mum and Dad walked in. I was waiting for them to order me to get out of the new bird's house, but they just smiled at each other and practically ignored me. I had steeled myself to make a stand, to protest against them donating my stuff to this new bird. I was ready to hook my toenails around the bars should they try to winkle me out, but to add to my confusion, Mum came over to give me a biscuit and told me I was a very good boy.

After several days, the big bird house stayed empty, so I assumed that the smelly emu had decided not to take up residence after all. I was full of relief, and having got used to its house, I decided that I would use it as my regular daytime bed. I always slept upstairs at night, but during the day, I took to sleeping in the bird house.

Mum and Dad were obviously ok with this, as they sometimes even shut the door and spread one of my blankets over one end of it. It was actually quite a cosy little den in there and I started to like it. There was even a special water bowl that fixed to the side of the house so that I could lift up my head and have a drink without bothering myself to walk over to my normal bowls. There was enough room to stand up and stretch, turn around and sprawl right out, so I was happy to spend time in there, even when the door was shut.

Sometimes I would stay in the bird house with the door shut when Mum and Dad were in the garden, and a few times, they even went out for 5 minutes to the shop for milk and I didn't mind too much. Obviously they got the same enthusiastic greeting when they came in, whether they had been at the shop up the road for 5 minutes, or in the garden for 2 hours. We hounds are like that. You will get greeted just as enthusiastically no matter where you have been, or how long you have been gone. It's a pack bonding thing you know. We simply love you.

Chapter 26

HOME ALONE

As I said, after getting used to MY bird house, I was quite ok about having the door shut and being left alone for a little while. However, Mum and Dad started to leave me in there for longer periods of time and I wasn't sure that I liked where this was going.

Mum started going off to work in the mornings without me and I would be shut in the birdhouse.

She would pop back home after a couple of hours and once I had calmed myself down, she would open the door and I would be able to go and play for a while. Then she would ask me to get back into the bird house, give me a biscuit and go back to work. I didn't mind going back into it, as it was big enough to have a little game in and was actually very comfy. However, I did get rather lonely when she left me and I worried constantly about her and Dad and if they were ok without me.

Sometimes I would amuse myself and pass the time by singing. I heard the neighbours telling Mum about me singing one day over the fence. Do you know, she only went and apologised to them! What a blooming cheek, I have a fine singing voice! Anyway, they said they didn't mind and that they understood that I was a bit lonely, which was very nice of them.

I still got to go to work with Mum most days, but I was now part time and my hours were getting cut shorter each week. I supposed it was to get me used to my impending redundancy. I was getting used to being home alone, but I certainly didn't like it that much.

Us hounds are pack creatures and not really designed to be left all alone. It is a lot to ask of us, but we do it to please you. We do our best to fit in with your busy lives and try to understand because we love and respect you, but we are much happier when you return home and our pack is together again.

As I was being left home alone more and more, Mum and Dad went out and bought two sets of half glass panelled double doors to separate the three rooms downstairs.

The back room was our main evening 'den' where we snuggled up together to watch the TV box. The middle room was where I had my daytime bird house bed, which conveniently, was also where the food was prepared. The other room at the front was where the birds lived.

As I mentioned before, the birds were strictly off limits to me and I was not allowed near them when I was alone in the house. I wasn't allowed in the TV box room on my own either for some reason. Maybe it was due to the indoor tree trunk munching incident. (I later found out it was called a coffee table).

Dad soon set about the task of fitting the doors and after much banging, 'naughty Dad words', a box of plasters and several dozen cups of tea, both sets of doors were in place, and my daytime kennel had expanded greatly.

Chapter 27

THE KITCHEN DEMOLITION

One day, Mum and Dad went out and didn't close the birdhouse door. The other big, wooden doors were closed though.

I sat there for a minute, wondering what to do, then decided to check out the kitchen for crumbs and morsels. Despite thoroughly licking the surfaces (giraffe legs are useful sometimes), I hadn't really found anything worth mentioning on the worktops or draining board. However, I did manage to winkle out a piece of dried, fluffy pasta that had somehow got wedged in between the washing machine and the dishwasher. It was quite a find, and I was very pleased with myself at having the intelligence and skills that were required to retrieve it. My paws are quite big, but can be very dextrous when they need to be.

I went back to my bed in the birdhouse and laid there listening to the radio music box. I would much prefer to listen to a channel that spoke my own language, but Mum and Dad meant well, and I suppose I did find human voices a little comforting when I was alone, even if they were strangers and not my own pack members.

After a short time, Mum and Dad came back in, and once I had got over the initial excitement and had performed the ritual slobbery greetings, they made a huge fuss of me and told me I was a very good boy.

The next day the same thing happened and they went out and left me. This time they were gone for longer and I was starting to get bored. There were no more bits of pasta and I had played with all my toys, so I had a little sing song to keep myself cheerful. When they came in, I was told I was a good boy again, and later on we went for our usual walkies.

The next day came and off they went again. I wasn't too happy about this, as they were making rather a habit of going out without me; however, before she went out, Mum had given me a hard, red, plastic ball, which was stuffed full of bits of my favourite biscuit. I took my mind off of feeling lonely and worrying about my pack, by chasing the ball around the kitchen for the next hour or so. It was very hard to get the biscuits out, so I had to resort to pinning it down with my paws and chewing a big hole in the thing in order to get to them. It was worth the effort though, as it was full.

After a little 'post snack nap', I began to wonder how much longer they would be gone. The more I thought about it, the more upset I became. Suppose something bad had happened to them? Suppose my pack was in danger and I wasn't there to protect them? I started pacing around, listening out for any signs that they were about to return, but nothing. Panic took over and I decided I had to do something.

I proceeded to frantically try and dig and chew my way out through the big doors so that I could go and rescue them. It was hard work and my paws and teeth ached, and I seemed to be getting nowhere fast.

I decided to try elsewhere, but after trying to dig and chew through the new panelled doors (both sets), the floorboards, skirting boards, two walls and the kitchen worktop, I realised that I was trapped. I was unable to escape to rescue my poor Mum and Dad.

I was so stressed and desperately needed the loo (nerves and all those biscuits I suppose), but despite my high state of anxiety, I remembered the 'ALL deposits must be made in the garden only' rule, so I held onto it, which, under those extremely stressful circumstances, is something I was very proud of. I was such a good dog. No wonder Mum and Dad loved me so much.

After what seemed like an eternity (actually it was only about 3 hours, but it seemed much longer), I heard the key in the front door. They were home, safe at last.

Obviously I was beside myself with relief that they were ok and that nothing bad had happened after all. Pack members, even the Alphas are sometimes killed during a hunt you know. I was leaping around, whining with relief and joy, but for some reason, Mum and Dad did not tell me I was a good boy this time. They just stood there staring at each other and looking around the kitchen. It was most odd, because Mum's face went pale and Dad's went red. They were like a pair of Chameleons changing skin tones.

Dad started to shake, and Mum quickly opened the back door, and I gratefully rushed out to make my long overdue deposit. I was sure that I would be told I was a good boy after that, but as I went to go back in, I found that the door was shut and there was a lot of commotion going on inside. Mum and Dad were making an awful lot of racket in there. I heard lots of shouting and banging around. I wondered what on earth could be wrong. Something bad must have happened while they were out, that's why they were so late home. Poor Mum and Dad, I wished that there was something I could have done to help. They were obviously trying to shield me from the problem by making me wait outdoors. How sweet of them. They were so thoughtful.

At least I had done my bit and been a good boy by remembering the 'all deposits outside' rule, otherwise they would have had to clear up after me, and that would have made their already bad day even worse.

After a long time, I was let in, but despite my best attempts at inducing a fuss, they still virtually ignored me all evening. I was very upset and confused. Humans are such strange, complex creatures. I don't think I will ever understand them.

The next day when Mum and Dad went out, for some reason they shut me in the birdcage. It was back to square one again.

However, there were more, bigger and exciting changes to come. It was with great interest that I overheard one particular conversation soon after my attempts to break out of the kitchen to rescue Mum and Dad……….

Chapter 28

PROBLEM SOLVED OR DOUBLE TROUBLE?

Despite several attempts at leaving my birdcage door open for short times, I would still occasionally get anxious for my pack's safety and would try to escape to go and look for them. Some days I could cope ok, but on other days, something would trigger a panic attack and I would frantically try to chew and dig my way out of the kitchen.

For some reason, Mum very kindly started coating my usual attempted escape routes with all sorts of tasty stuff, like onion, mustard and vinegar, which was very thoughtful of her really, as it made the necessary chewing so much more interesting. I thoroughly enjoyed the different flavourings, though I must admit that the chilli stuff put me off a bit till I got used to it.

Even though Mum always came home every day to let me in the garden and give me my lunch, both her and Dad agreed that it was rather unfair to leave me alone in the house for such a long time each day. They didn't want me, or them, to keep having to go through all that stress of me chewing and digging in the kitchen.

Of course, there was never any question of me being taken back to the kennels. I was far too loveable and an established, valued member of the pack.

Eventually, the birdcage was folded flat and put in the shed for storage. The sofa bed that was usually in the front room, was put in the kitchen in its place, so it then became officially all mine!

Mum warned me that if I decided to chew it up, I would not get another one, so I left it well alone. However, one day when I was extra bored, I had great fun shredding the little cushions that sat on it. It was so much fun, and it looked just like it had been snowing in the kitchen by the time Mum came home. It was like Christmas all over again!

The most exciting thing that had recently become under much discussion, was the pros and cons of introducing another dog to our pack. Of course this never failed to attract my attention, and the old radars would hone in on every word during this particular debate.

It seemed that Mum was trying to persuade Dad into agreeing to have another dog. Her main argument for getting another dog was that it would resolve my anxiety problems. Dad's argument against this was that he was worried that by adding another dog to our pack, it would simply be creating 'double trouble'. He also pointed out that there was the added expense of maintaining another pack member, which was fair comment I suppose, as I was a bit spoilt and any new addition would be too.

Mum counteracted this by pointing out that it was going to cost a fortune to keep repairing the kitchen, and that a fellow canine would ease my loneliness and worries, and ultimately, my welfare was priority.

Dad was also worried about lack of space in our small den, but Mum would then point out that for such leggy, large dogs, we fold up small and take up very little space. We are happy to lie quietly out of the way, as long as we are given access to comfy beds.

As poor Dad started to buckle and weaken, the discussion was swiftly moved on (by Mum, naturally) to what type of dog might join our pack. The possibility of getting a smaller dog was discussed, then dismissed, as both Mum and Dad agreed that I would need a companion with similar characteristics to myself (bone idle) and not some lively little whippersnapper that would expect me to play all day.

Much to my relief, a larger lively dog was also a big No No. I thought about living permanently 24/7 with a dog like my friends, Pogo and Pola and shuddered at the mere thought. I would probably not even last a week! As much as I loved them, an hour or two in their company in any one day was more than enough for me.

After several weeks of discussions, it was finally decided that our pack would be increased by 1 x Greyhound, and it would probably be a young lady. Needless to say, I was like a dog with two tails (normal tails though, not psychotic ones; one psychotic tail was more than enough to cope with!).

Once my initial excitement had died down, little doubts started to creep in. On the plus side, I would no longer be lonely when Mum and Dad were out, and I would have someone to play with.

One the minus side, once the new pack member arrived, I would have to share my time with Mum and Dad, my sofa, my fusses, my garden and even more disturbing, my toys and treats.

I decided there and then that I would not, under any circumstances, share my treats, or my beloved Teds. Teds is my cherished soft and cuddly night time bear that Aunty Debs bought for me, and he went to bed with me every night. I would gently carry him up to bed and refuse to go up the wooden hill without him. He was mine and nobody else would get their paws on him!

There was nothing else for it. I would have to set the new pack member straight as soon as she arrived. I would outline her place in the pack, just like Dad attempts to do with Mum, but unlike Dad, I would make a proper job of it! The welfare of my beloved Teds and all of my other toys depended on it.

I decided that I would just relax and enjoy my limited time as an only pup, whilst also looking forward to a whole new exciting chapter in my life with another hound soon to be joining my pack. And hopefully it would be a fit looking girl!

Chapter 29

INTERNET DATING

After visiting my old kennels at Old Windsor and finding that there were no suitable girls in residence at that time, with the help of Mum, I turned my paw to internet dating.

We found a picture of Fleur, a gorgeous looking girl who had recently retired from her racing career. She was staying at a retired Greyhound kennels, so we arranged to meet her on the way to visit our Kent pack one day.

Of course I was very excited. I had never been on a blind date before and wondered what she was like in the fur, if you know what I mean.

When we got to the kennels, I was feeling a bit overwhelmed because I had never seen so many Greyhounds all in one place before.

Most of them were barking at me and I must admit to feeling a little scared.

As you know, I am a Lurcher, which means that I am of mixed parentage. I am only half Greyhound, the other half of me is Saluki, and these Greyhounds had only ever seen fellow purebreds before. They were not sure what to make of me at all.

Soon after we arrived, a nice lady appeared with the good looking girl that we had seen in the picture. She was certainly a well built, powerful looking girl, and was almost as tall as me.

This was not a problem, as my old Mastiff girlfriend at the kennels (as you already know), was much bigger than me. I liked my gals well padded!

I went up to say hello to her, but she lunged forward and snapped at my face. I was a bit shocked and immediately backed off to hide behind Dad's legs.

We went for a little walk down the lane together and I tried to be nice to her, but she was having none of it and kept curling her lip at me. She didn't seem to want to know me at all.

Obviously I felt very dejected, but true to my breed, was not going to give up that easily. When we arrived back at the kennels, Mum and Dad told the kennel lady what had happened, and they decided to let us both off lead in the paddock to see if we would play together. After having several knock backs, I was quite terrified of this lady, and was secretly very relieved when she had a muzzle put on.

After a while, she wasn't quite so aggressive towards me and we did have a little game of sorts, but my confidence had been knocked quite badly. I was still scared of her and she knew it.

It wasn't her fault. Poor girl had only just retired from racing and was still very stressed, so I suppose it was to be expected. It shook me up a bit though I can tell you.

Initially, Mum and Dad agreed that subject to a home check, we would bring this feisty lady home and try to get her settled into our pack. However, after more thought and lots of discussions during the day, they realised that sadly, me and Fleur were simply not compatible, and that I would quite possibly have to live the rest of my life in fear of her.

First thing the next morning, Mum rang the kennels. She apologised and said that they had given it much thought, and had decided that Fleur really wasn't the right girl to join our pack. My happiness must come first, and it wouldn't have been fair to her, me or any of us if she came to live with us.

Mum and Dad were sorry to have had to make that decision, but although I was a bit sad that this gorgeous looking girl was not moving in, I was actually greatly relieved. As beautiful as she was, she scared me half to death, and there was no way that I would have had the bottle to tell her not to touch my Teds. He could have been ripped apart at the seams and I would have had no choice but to watch helplessly. She needed a much tougher guy than me that's for sure. I'm just a big old softie and too nice for my own good sometimes.

Although Fleur was totally unaware that she was ever even under discussion, Mum felt terrible, as if she had let her down in some way. To be honest, Fleur probably thought that Mum and Dad were just another new bunch of volunteer walkers that were taking her out for a walk that day. We kept checking back on the website, and were very pleased to see that this beautiful lady soon found a good home, but it was back to the drawing board for us.

We were looking on the computer again one day, when we found a website for a Greyhound rescue in Essex, called Castledon kennels.

There were pictures of each resident, along with a little story telling you about them and what sort of new home they would like to go to.

There were a few lovely looking girls there, and one or two caught my eye, but after my other scary experience, we decided to send an email about me and my personality and leave it up to the people at the kennels to see if they could help. We hoped that one of their girls, or even boys, might be a suitable companion for me.

I didn't really mind if another boy came to join the pack, but I was keeping all four paws crossed that it was going to be a cute, pretty girl. I am a bit of a ladies pup you know.

Imagine our excitement when we received a reply from a lovely lady at the kennels called Jodie, saying that she could help us.

We were soon to find out that Jodie is rather an expert on canine match-making, and could give that Cilla woman a run for her money! Jodie told me and Mum, that she had the perfect girl there to share my 'forever sofa'. The young lady in question was a dainty Irish girl called Speck. She was one of the girls that I had thought looked very sweet and pretty, but also had a sad look in her beautiful eyes too.

Jodie said that Speck had come over from Ireland as a failed racer. She said that she was very shy and sweet natured and had unfortunately suffered abuse in the past. She felt that Speck would benefit from living with a confident but kind and understanding chap just like me and that I would help her to re-build her confidence.

In return, I would have a beautiful, inoffensive and loyal companion to share my lonely days with.

Although we hadn't actually met, I immediately felt protective towards her, and knew that she would pose no threat to Teds or me.

And so our blind date was arranged. I just couldn't wait to meet her!

Chapter 30

THE ONE

I have heard humans say that when you meet your soul mate, you just know that they are 'The One'. Well, you may be shocked to learn that you humans do not have the monopoly on this wonderful force of nature. It can also happen to us dogs and other animals too. It certainly happened to me on the day that I first met Speck.

It was the 28th of June, and against my wishes, I had just been subjected to a vile bath. I was frantically rolling around shedding out the loose hair and drying myself off on Mum and Dad's duvet and pillows, when suddenly, out of the blue, I had this wonderful feeling of peace and wellbeing wash over me. Maybe it was just relief that the terrible, tortuous bathing session was over with, but I couldn't help feeling that it was going to be a very good day indeed.

The old twizzle was starting to frizz up, but luckily it was my summer twizzle, so laying on it till it dried should keep it in check. The same method could be applied to the fluffy knickers too.

As I lay there on my back, twizzle firmly tucked under my leg, the sunlight was streaming into the room and onto my face. I felt myself drifting off to a warm, floaty, faraway place, where food was plentiful, and small furry things that were kept specifically for chasing purposes, were running loose everywhere.

I had almost descended into full slumber, when I was rudely snapped back into reality by Mum suddenly appearing in the bedroom doorway angrily ordering my hairy, smelly, wet butt off of the bed, her words not mine.

I sulkily got off and padded over to my own bed to complete the drying process, but the majority of water and dead hair had already been liberally deposited all over Mum and Dad's bed, so there wasn't much left to do. Just the twizzle left to deal with really.

I don't like getting told off one little bit, and will admit to being a bit of a sulky pants when it does happen. Despite my rugged, macho exterior, I am a very sensitive chap and really do take things to heart; but nothing was going to keep me down for long that day. I was going to meet the girl of my dreams in a few short hours and I was on top of the world. And I smelt nice too.

At last the time came to make the journey to meet my girl and I couldn't get in the car quick enough. Both Mum and Dad remarked at my unusual enthusiasm to leap aboard. They said that I must have known what was going on. Durrr, of course I knew. I'm not stupid! Normally, due to my 'delicate tummy problems', I have to be coaxed or ordered into the car, but I had other, much more important things than vomiting on my mind.

It was a hot day though, and despite having both of the sunroofs open, I did start to feel a bit queasy during the journey. I started to panic that I would have to meet my intended, covered in stinky vomit and carrots, so I decided to stretch my neck up and stick my nose right out of the sunroof.

The fresh air worked wonders, and my tummy soon settled back down to where it should be. The only problem was, the air rushing into my nostrils at such high speed, induced a violent sneezing fit and the whole interior of the car, including me, Mum and Dad, got showered with Sonic snot. It was most invigorating though, you should try it sometime.

By the time we arrived at Jodie's house, the product of my mucous membranes had dried and flaked off of its hosts, though I noticed that Mum still had a bit in the back of her hair.

I looked good and still smelt good too, which was the main thing. After all, it was MY special day.

When we got there, I was eager to go and meet Speck, but she hadn't arrived from the kennels yet, so we sat and waited in the car. I had heard that it was customary for the lady to keep her date waiting for a little while. It was only a few minutes, but it was the longest few minutes of my life and being so keen, we had arrived early.

My nerves were jangling, and I was in danger of losing my cool and making a complete idiot of myself. I had brought gifts of toys and treats for Speck, and some treats for her kennel mates, so I hoped that would tell her that I am a very thoughtful, caring young man.

A car pulled into the driveway and a lady got out and came over to our car. I was trying to peer into the back of her car, but couldn't quite see.

Jodie introduced herself and said that she just had to pop into the house to get something and would be right back.

Mum and Dad got out and opened my door. Unable to wait a moment longer, we walked over to Jodie's car. Suddenly, this stunningly beautiful face appeared in the back window.

Mum and Dad started to make those soppy noises that you humans make when you see something cute, pretty and sweet, but as our eyes met through the glass, all I could think was WOW!

The best way I can describe what happened to me at that precise moment, is to say that it was like I had been hit over the head with a huge pig's ear. It was a short, sharp shock, but was extremely plcasant and painless.

Speck was a very shy little thing and looked away. I realised that I had been standing there like a gangly, goofy love-struck teenager, staring unashamedly at this beautiful girl without blinking. I also realised at that very moment that she was……..

THE ONE!

Chapter 31

OUR FIRST DATE

Jodie was soon back at the car and we all waited while she opened the door. Out popped this dinky, extremely pretty little lady, and it was immediately obvious why she was called Speck. Her beautiful black coat was liberally decorated with tiny white specks. She had the loveliest brown eyes that I had ever seen, though I could immediately see the fear and sadness in them. I wanted to reassure her that there was no need to be afraid, and that I would look after her. We all would.

I cautiously went over to say hello and we touched noses. My tail immediately exploded into windmill butt mode and was rapidly accelerating to the snake, when Mum told me I had to calm down or I might frighten Speck. Of course she was right. This timid little lady had obviously had a very rough time in the past and needed to be handled gently. The last thing she needed was to have some lumbering great giraffe scaring her to death. I tried to keep my tail in check, but as you know, it does its own thing, and I was beside myself with happiness and excitement. I had just met the love of my life and calm was not an option.

Jodie suggested that we all go for a walk in the paddock together, as this would calm me down and Speck and I could get to know each other a bit better.

Jodie waited in the house. She said to take as long as we wanted.

As we walked in the paddock, Speck started to look for me and seemed to want to walk next to me all the time. She didn't say a lot, but she was painfully shy and a bit scared, so I didn't take offence. I felt very comfortable with her and instinctively knew that she wasn't going to suddenly take a snap at me if I snuffled in her ears.

I love snuffling in ears. Of course, I love butt sniffing too. What? Hey, it's what we dogs all do! We think that some of the things you humans do are revolting, but we respect that you have your weird ways and we don't pull you up on them.

Anyway, as I was saying, ear snuffling is a great way to make friends, so I decided to be bold and make my move. I stuck my nose in her left ear and had a good old snuffle around. To my delight, she seemed to love it and leaned her head over so that I could delve a bit deeper. This was MY girl alright! I bet she would enjoy a good nibbling around her head and neck too, but decided that it might be a bit too much too soon. It was only our first date after all, and I am a Gentleman you know.

We spent a glorious half an hour or so walking in the paddock together, and I couldn't wait to take Speck back with us to show her round her new home and teach her the ropes and routines. She would love being a member of our pack, I just knew it.

As we made our way back to the house, I suddenly realised, that the decision as to whether Speck came home with us, was not mine to make, or hers. It was up to Mum and Dad.

With this awful thought in mind, I made sure that Mum and Dad noticed me making a big fuss of Speck and that she seemed to like me too.

When we got back to the house, Jodie came out and I put my radars on high alert. This discussion was the one that would decide whether my lovely Speck came home to live with me, or whether she went back to the kennels and I went home alone.

Jodie asked how we got on, and to my relief, Mum and Dad said that we all loved Speck. She was a sweetheart and she seemed to bond with me a little, so they would be very happy and honoured to have Speck come home and join our pack; if she wanted to of course.

Speck and I looked at each other, and though she was much too shy to say, I knew that she wanted to come home and live with me, as much as I wanted her to.

There was a lot more chat going on, but I had heard all that I needed to hear, so I relaxed and just enjoyed standing close to my lovely girl. I couldn't resist sneaking another cheeky ear snuffle, which she enjoyed as much as I did.

As I stood there, looking at Speck, feeling all luvved up and planning our first evening together, the old radars picked up on something that brought all my plans crashing to the ground. Speck would not be coming home with us that day. She had to return to the kennels and get 'booked in'. After it was done,

Jodie would bring her to us in a week or so, once she had recovered.

I realised that she was probably going to have her assets removed, just like I did. I really felt for her, but accepted that this was obviously the price we dogs all had to pay to live a life of luxury and happiness.

I didn't have the heart to tell her what was going to happen. I would just make extra fuss of her when she came home to try to make up for it. Obviously I was devastated that she couldn't come home with us right there and then, but I knew that she would be home soon, and we had the rest of our lives together to look forward to.

We said our goodbyes and I sent a private telepathic message to Speck. I told her that she was the most beautiful, sweet and lovely girl that I had ever met and that I couldn't wait for her to come home to me. I assured her that everything would be fine and told her not to worry. Nobody would ever hurt her again.

The last thing I said was that I would see her very soon and that I would be thinking about her all the time.

As she was led back to Jodie's car, she looked back at me and shyly conveyed two of the most wonderful telepathic words I had ever heard in my life. She said............

Me too.

Chapter 32

THE LONG WAIT

After my wonderful date with Speck, I could barely think of anything else, except dinner, walkies and my toys of course.

A few days later, we heard that thankfully, Speck's operation had gone ok and that she was fine, but she needed some time to recover. Apparently the 'pre-happiness' operation was much more serious for girls than it was for boys. I found this very hard to believe. I could hardly walk for two days, so what must my poor little Speck be feeling like if this was true?

I sent her several telepathic 'get well soon' messages every day, though I wasn't sure if she could receive them from that distance. I never got any back, so it was doubtful, but I still sent them anyway, just in case. Sadly, we were too far away to go and visit her.

While we were waiting for the big day when Speck would come home, we all made frequent trips to one of my favourite places in the world. The pet shop. We bought toys, a brush, had collar tags engraved, and collected various little bits and pieces to make Speck feel welcome. Mum had taken Speck's neck measurements, and her collar was on order. We got our collars custom made by a lovely lady who sells them on the internet. Mine is a very cool, macho 'pirate hound' design in red, with black satin lining (very appropriate for an avid bin raider). Speck's is a girly, pink, glittery one, with a sparkly dragonfly design and pink satin lining. Mum said she had to have a pretty collar because she was such a pretty girl, and Speck would love it, but me and Dad think its YUCK!

Now when we all go out, Dad always insists on holding my lead, as he doesn't like to hold Speck's girly pink one, which I think is fair enough. If they ever put it on me, I will refuse point blank to set paw out of the door! When he has to take us both out without Mum, he has no choice, but often mutters something like "should have got a pirate one for her too".

It was decided that during the day, Speck would share my sofa, and at night she would sleep next to me. Mum bought a double duvet and another single one. She folded the double one in half and put our 2 single ones side by side on top. It was a really big, comfy bed. I was looking forward to cuddling up to Speck at night.

I loved my dear Teds and explained to him that for his own safety, he wouldn't be able to sleep with me once Speck arrived. Besides, she might think I was a total wussy pansy taking my teddy to bed. Also, Teds is very precious to me. I look on him as my puppy, and I just couldn't bear to share him with anyone.

Everything was ready for the big day. All we could do now was wait. I was counting down the days when Speck would be coming home, but it seemed to be taking forever. Although it was only 10 days, it was quite possibly the longest wait of my life.

Chapter 33

THE DAY THAT SPECK CAME HOME

The big day that we had all been waiting for finally came. It was Sunday the 8th July, and my lady was coming home at last! I was very nervous, but happy.

Dad had to work later that afternoon, but Mum would be home, and they had both booked the next 2 weeks off to settle Speck into her new home.

We were all very excited, especially me!

Mum and Dad tried to calm me down and wear me out with a run and a long walk, but as much as they tried not to show it in front of me, they were very excited too and I could feel their vibes.

I realised that the time was getting close, because Mum kept peering out of the front window, obviously waiting for Jodie's car. Dad told her to sit down and relax, but every time a car stopped outside, we would all (Dad included), pop our heads up. How could they possibly expect me to remain calm when they were just as bad?

After what seemed an eternity, Mum shouted "they're here!" I went into manic panic mode and was almost bouncing off the walls. Dad was trying to get me to wait in the kitchen, but I was having none of it. After chasing me around the ground floor of the house several times trying to grab my collar without success, he resorted to shouting at me to get my attention. (Well, have you ever tried to catch a Lurcher that is in a high state of excitement?)

Dad used to be in the army and when he shouts, you either cease the offensive behaviour, or risk getting damaged eardrums. I value all of my senses, so ceased my offensive behaviour and sulkily padded over to him. He told me to wait there and closed the doors. It was so unfair. I had waited all this time and I just wanted to be first at the door to welcome my Speck to her new home.

As I leapt up and down at the glass door, I realised that Dad was right. I was way too hyper and over the top and could well scare her half to death, but I just couldn't seem to stop myself from bouncing!

As the front door swung open, I could see Jodie smiling and talking to Mum and Dad, but I couldn't see Speck. I was about to start worrying that I had been stood up and she wasn't coming after all, when I spotted her taking her first tentative steps inside her new home. She looked as beautiful as I remembered her to be, but the poor girl also looked absolutely terrified.

I remembered how scared I was when I first set paw in the house. It was like landing on a different planet. It had taken me a while to get used to the noises, machines and routines, and I was much more brave, outgoing and relaxed than poor Speck. She was a terribly nervous little thing, so this must have been even more terrifying for her than it was for me. With this in mind, I made a conservative effort to calm myself down. I needed to be calm and strong to make her feel safe in this strange new world. So I quit the bouncing, and sat whimpering pathetically instead.

As Speck nervously walked into the living room, she spotted me through the glass door panels and gave me a shy look. Her eyes were huge like saucers as she looked around, trying to take in and make some sense of all these strange new sights and smells. She looked up at Jodie for a bit of reassurance and it was given to her immediately. Speck trusted Jodie and wanted to stay close to her. I felt sad that poor Speck was so terrified, and wanted to tell her that she would be ok and that nothing or nobody here would ever hurt her.

After a little while, Dad opened the doors so that I could go and say hello. I had been very patient and calm, but as soon as the doors were opened, I lost all my suave coolness and rushed over to welcome my beautiful girl. The sight of a large, gangly beast hurtling towards you at high speed would scare anyone half to death, and in her state of anxiety, Speck was petrified. I was so sorry that I had frightened her, and I knew that I would have to calm right down before she would want to get near me again.

Mum kept me on my lead after that, so that I didn't forget myself again and make any sudden moves to try and play with Speck and scare her any further. We all went into the garden, and Speck was let off the lead to have a sniff round and explore her new garden. She seemed to calm down once outside and even seemed to be enjoying checking out her new surroundings.

I just wanted to play, but we had the rest of our lives to play, so I stayed on my lead and let her wander around in peace.

Eventually, we all went back indoors, and Mum suggested that Jodie coax Speck up the wooden hill so that she would see that there was nothing scary up there. In fact, our lovely comfy duvets and treat jar were up there next to Mum and Dad's bed, so it was all good things up the wooden hill.

Of course, the one scary thing that Speck did have to confront was the wooden hill itself. Having never seen a wooden hill before, she was understandably quite scared and unsure, but as she trusted Jodie, she followed her up and had a look around.

Getting back down is much scarier than going up, and because we have such long legs, it is a skill that is only perfected with time and practice. I must say, that Speck's first attempt, though not the most graceful scene to witness, was very impressive and even rather elegant compared to my first clumsy, half gallop, half roll, pinball-like descent, which had resulted in me bouncing off the front door and the radiator, before being jettisoned through the front room doorway and landing in an undignified heap right in front of the birds. I swear I heard that rotten Jack parrot laughing at me.

There was a bit more chat between Jodie, Mum and Dad, and some papers changed hands. I remembered that we had to do all this when I joined the pack a year earlier. I don't pretend to understand what all the fuss is over these papers, but I do know that once they had been handed over to Mum and Dad, the pack membership was definite and final. Speck was now officially a member of our pack and no longer a resident at Castledon kennels.

Soon after the papers had been exchanged, Jodie said goodbye to Speck, and gave her a big hug and a kiss and then she was gone.

Although it was a very happy and exciting day for us, it was also a very scary and traumatic day for poor Speck. Her one and only trusted friend had just left her with strangers, in very alien surroundings and she was panic stricken.

Like me, Speck had never set foot inside a house before. Jodie was quite tearful when she left. She had nursed Speck back to health and gained her trust. Speck had quite obviously been abused by wicked people in her past, but she trusted Jodie completely. They had spent many months together and they loved each other. Now all of a sudden, Speck was alone in a strange place with a strange pack and she was terrified.

Dad had to go off to work, so it was just me, Speck, Mum and the birds. For the next few hours, Speck was like a jelly, trembling and panting constantly. She kept running over to the window whenever a car stopped outside, to see if Jodie had come back for her. Her little ears would sag and she looked so sad, disappointed and dejected when she realised that it wasn't Jodie, and she would slowly turn and move away. It was very sad and heart breaking to watch.

Mum had a few tears, but not in front of Speck as she didn't want to make her anxiety any worse.

Mum decided to use Speck's great love of food to try to calm her down and win her over. She distracted her by offering small treats, and of course, I had some too.

Eventually, after a while, as Jodie had predicted, Speck stopped pacing and started to take notice of her new surroundings for the first time since Jodie had left her.

I was allowed off the lead and we both went out into the garden for a walk around and a sniff. I did try to play with Speck, but she told me firmly and in no uncertain terms, that she was not ready to play just yet. I got the message and backed off and just followed her around. Poor girl was having a very stressful day, but she would come round in time and play with me.

Everything was going well and dinner time came around at last. Speck had her own food bowl and stand which was on the other side of the kitchen to mine. Mum put my food bowl in my stand, and made me wait while she put Speck's one in hers. The second that Mum had moved away from Speck's bowl, she was there like a flash. She gobbled her dinner down before I had even got halfway through mine. I am not a slow eater myself, but I was so impressed at this girl's appetite. However, my admiration turned to panic as she suddenly rushed past Mum and lunged towards my dinner bowl. She was going to try to eat mine too!

Mum shouted "NO Speck!" and at the same time, I told her off with a loud bark and barged her away. As much as I loved her, some things would remain sacred and personal, and my dinner was one of them. Teds of course was another. I had to tell her that stealing my food was most definitely out of order.

This scared poor Speck so much that she quite literally screamed and ran up the wooden hill to hide.

Mum waited for a few minutes and then called her a few times. She was obviously not going to come down, so after a few more minutes, Mum went up to see if she was ok. The poor girl was so frightened that she started to scream as soon as Mum went near her. She had even wee'd on the floor because she was so scared. Mum was understandably upset that Speck thought she was going to get a beating, but Mum understood that she didn't know her yet, and was scared of all strangers. So, trying not to let it show, Mum sat on the floor and didn't look at her. She just sat talking quietly to her, and eventually, Speck calmed down and even went over to her for a little fuss.

After a while, they both came down and I went over to say sorry for scaring her. Mum apologised to us both. She said it wasn't Speck's fault, or mine, but hers. She promised to guard my dinner more carefully until Speck learnt the house rules.

Once she was sure that we were ok together, she went off up the hill with a bucket of soapy smelling water and gloves, to clean up the soggy consequence of poor Speck's terrible panic attack.

During the evening, Speck's trembling and panting became less noticeable, which we took as a good sign. She seemed more nervous when we went towards her, or tried to touch her, and she would scream and run away if we moved too quickly or suddenly near her. Because of this, we left her alone to rest on the sofa. Mum spoke to her every now and then, and persuaded her to come over to us for a treat.

Later in the evening, Dad came home and I rushed over to greet him as usual.

Speck didn't move. Another pack member arriving in the den just seemed to start off her nerves again. Mum explained to Dad that it would be best to leave Speck alone, and after a while she calmed down again. Once she was less scared, Dad offered her a treat and she warily came over to him to get it. He stroked her head and she ran off to the sofa to eat it.

Jodie had told us that Speck was in a bad way when she first arrived at the kennels, and it was obviously going to be a long process getting her to trust us all completely. She was a very brave girl though, and underneath all those bundles of nerves, there was a happy, playful little pup waiting to emerge.

We all vowed that we would help her in any way we could, to lay her traumatic past to rest once and for all, so that she could enjoy the rest of her life with us.

On a serious note, me and Mum would just like to deviate for a moment, to stress that If you haven't already got a houseful of beautiful Sighthounds, and you are seriously contemplating taking up the honour of sharing your home and life with one or more of us exquisite creatures, please do not be put off by Speck's behaviour at this time, as her case is not the norm. Unfortunately, there are other poor dogs out there in rescue centres like Speck, that have been badly treated by humans, but the vast majority of Greyhounds up for adoption, are normal, stable, well adjusted, friendly dogs, who have simply been rejected from the racing kennels for one reason or another. They just need a kind family to give them a home. Greyhounds adjust remarkably quickly, and will reward you with unconditional love for the rest of their lives.

Even very traumatised hounds like Speck, who need that little bit of extra time, patience, love and understanding, can be transformed into perfectly normal, well balanced pets given time and lots of tlc. Speck is now a normal, happy, rather bossy lady, who will even bark at people for attention if they dare to ignore her!

As for my demolition skills, I only applied them in the very early days when I was suffering from separation anxiety, and didn't understand my new house and pack rules and routines. Again, this is not normal behaviour.

So please don't think that your new pack member will automatically behave as me or Speck did when we first went to live with our Mum and Dad.

The staff at the rescue kennels will always advise you on the characteristics and behaviour of the many hounds that are always waiting for new homes, and help you to find the right hound to suit your pack. Giving a home to any unwanted animal is extremely rewarding, and any kind, caring person can do this, but you must be in it for the long haul and be prepared for a few 'teething problems'.

If you are willing and able to take on one of the more troubled little souls, in time you will eventually bear witness to the miracle of seeing your terrified little friend, slowly transforming into the happy, confident, unique individual that he or she has never before had the chance to be.

Obviously, the early days can be very upsetting and distressing at times, and it is not for everyone, and certainly not for the faint-hearted! It is a huge commitment, and for someone that loves animals, re-habilitating a traumatised dog can be traumatising for the person too, but the end results are so worth it

You will need to remain calm and confident at all times, and you must resist the urge to rush over to the poor animal to comfort him/her every time he/she has a panic attack over something trivial that most dogs would not bat an eyelid at, as this only aggravates the problem.

Be patient and persevere and you will win in the end.

Mum and Dad are normal people (well, some may beg to differ!), seriously, I mean that they are not dog trainers, but with common sense, and invaluable tips and advice from books, TV programmes, the internet and of course the rescue kennels, we all helped to provide Speck with the emotional tools that she needed to fight and defeat her demons, and become a normal, well-adjusted girl.

If we can do it, anyone can!

Anyway, back to Speck's first day at home............

We were left in the back living room with Dad, watching the TV box while Mum fed the birds and let them out for a fly in the front room.

After a while, she came in with cups of tea for her and Dad and another small treat for us, and we all just sat for a while. Speck still didn't want to join in for cuddles, so we left her in peace, but we noticed that she was looking more interested in our group hugs. We did offer her a place on the big sofa with us, but she declined. Mum went to stroke her, but she just looked scared again, so we felt it best to leave her to come to us when she felt the time was right for her. I think she was starting to realise that Mum and Dad would not hurt her though, because she could see that I was snuggled up between them having a cuddle. We all felt very sad that she was on the sofa on her own, but it was the best thing we could do for her at the time. She would come over when she was ready to join in. If we tried to force her to come over and join us for a cuddle, she would go into panic mode again. So it was a matter of letting her move at her own pace. After all it was only her first day.

After an exhausting, stressful day, it was time for a last wee, then off to bed, so me and Speck went out to the garden and did our biz, and once we were back in, Dad locked the door and we prepared ourselves for the next and final traumatic experience of the day....

Getting Speck up the wooden hill to bed.

Chapter 34

OUR FIRST NIGHT TOGETHER

I went up the wooden hill and Speck, after being coaxed with a bit of biscuit, eventually came up too without too much fuss, then Mum showed her to her bed.

Naturally, I had dreamed of the time that I would share my duvet with a stunningly beautiful girl, and couldn't quite believe the time had finally come. I wondered if she might want to snuggle, or if I should make the first move over to her, or would she inch her way over to me? The suspense was killing me. It's not something that you should ask a lady though is it. "Would you like to snuggle over here with me?" I decided to play it cool and see what she would do. I am a gentleman after all.

My question was soon answered, leaving no room for doubt as she immediately curled up on her side of the duvet and was asleep in no time at all. Oh well, the poor girl had had a very busy day.

I settled myself down for a good rest, comforted by the fact that she was obviously very tired, and would therefore be the perfect duvet mate, and would lay still and sleep soundly till the morning.

How wrong was I?!................................

I was woken several times during the night by Speck fidgeting and making weird noises in her sleep. She even kicked me up the butt a few times, but I didn't take it personally. I realised that she wasn't being nasty, she was asleep and unaware she was even doing it. She was just having bad dreams and was feeling very unsettled.

I remembered how that felt when everything was all strange for me, so I just moved a bit further away and tried to get some sleep. The trouble was, the farther away I moved, the nearer she moved to me, so in the end, I was wedged up against the wall and was getting pummelled by frantically scrabbling paws that were probably in hot pursuit of a rabbit.

This was not good and I was forced to vacate my bed and move round to Speck's half of the duvet. I was just getting comfy, when I realised that she was moving back towards me. It was going to be a very long night. I thought of what Dad often said to Mum and frankly had to agree.

Females always hog the duvet!

I was rudely awakened at 6am, after what I can only describe as a fitful, restless sleep of what seemed like 5 minutes, by Speck, who was obviously refreshed by her restful night of rabbit chasing and duvet hogging. She was mooching around, whining and pacing and wondering where her breakfast was. I tried to explain that we don't do early mornings in this kennel when Mum and Dad are on holiday, and that she should go back to bed for a couple more hours. She really didn't seem to understand though and very brazenly went straight over to Mum and Dad's bed and barked in Dad's face! If that wasn't bad enough, she then leapt straight on top of them both and barked again!

I cringed, waiting for one or both of them to grumpily shout "OFF!" or "BED!", but Dad just mumbled and retreated further under the duvet, and poor Mum sleepily emerged, put on her dressing gown and said "come on then". I of course, was reluctant to leave my bed at this unearthly hour, but Speck was wide awake and excitedly racing around. It was like a different dog had swapped places with Speck during the night. She was certainly not the same terrified girl that had moved in the day before.

Mum made me get up as well, and the three of us went down the hill. Speck was a bit unsteady, but managed it eventually. Mum let us in the garden and we did our first biz of the day. Mum made a huge fuss of Speck, and I remembered that I used to get the same amount of praise when I was learning to do biz in the garden. Just so I didn't feel left out, she gave me extra fuss too. My Mum was a nice Mum, even if she had just raked me out of my warm, comfy pit against my will!

Speck was getting very excited at the prospect of breakfast, but I just wanted to go back to bed for a while and so did Mum. Mum explained to Speck that she was a very good girl for remembering not to do any wees in the house and for waiting until she was let into the garden, but breakfast is not served in this kennel at 6am on any day! With that, me and Mum trudged back up the hill to go back to bed for a couple of hours. Speck stood at the bottom of the hill looking bewildered and disappointed. Mum almost caved in, but we both knew that if she had, then Speck would have us all up at 6am every morning, so I was relieved that Mum stayed strong and coaxed her back up and onto our bed. She seemed a bit upset and possible even a bit huffy, but after a bit of pacing around and whining, she decided to give up and went back to sleep, as we all did.

Poor Speck, it is hard for all of us hounds to learn new routines, but she would be ok. We had a good, safe and happy pack, and I knew that she would soon feel much better.

I was looking forward to the day when she felt relaxed and comfortable enough to want to have a game with me. I had tried a few times to induce play, but she seemed to misinterpret my playful advances, and all I got for my trouble was a frosty glare and even a snap once! I guess I would just have to be patient and let her tell me when she was ready to play with me.

Chapter 35

SPECK LEARNING THE ROPES

The next few days were spent gently easing Speck into our daily routines, and I must say that she was a fast learner. At first, if Mum or Dad made any sudden movements or noises near her, she would run off up the wooden hill screaming like a banshee. It was very sad and I hoped that she would soon realise that nobody would ever hurt her again.

I understood her actions completely though, as I had not had the best start in life either. I remember one time, when Mum had reached back to grab one of my toys to play with me, and she accidentally knocked me on the snout. It was only a very light touch, but it brought on a flashback from the past. I threw myself on the floor and tried to protect my head by curling up into a ball, and just screamed and screamed.

Poor Mum was devastated. It had been a perfectly innocent accident, which hadn't even hurt physically, but mentally, it had reduced me to a trembling, screaming wreck on the floor. The more she tried to comfort me, the louder I screamed and the tighter I curled up. In the end she had to walk off and wait for me to get a grip. She sat on the floor a few feet away, and once I stopped screaming and realised that there was nobody there that would hurt me, and that it had all been a silly mistake, I soon calmed down. It was a bad panic attack that was all.

As I looked into her tear filled eyes, I felt very bad

that I had upset her, and padded over to apologise and administer and receive reassuring cuddles that we both needed.

It never happened again.

Whenever Speck ran off up the hill, we would leave her alone for 10 minutes or so, and then Mum or Dad would stand at the foot of the hill and call her. If she did not appear, a rattle of her food dish or our treat tin was enough to get her back down.

Eventually, her bolting off up to her 'safe place' became less and less frequent, and after a few more days, once she felt more secure in general, Mum would shut the door so that Speck would have to face her fears and not get into the habit of running away from things. It might sound cruel, but it really was the best thing to do for her, otherwise she would spend the rest of her life running away in fear. This way, she had to 'deal with it' and eventually her confidence grew. Nowadays, she is as brazen and cheeky as me. Well, almost!

Mum and Dad were at home all day, every day with us for almost two weeks and it was lovely. Towards the end of the first week, Mum and Dad would go off out for a little while and leave Speck and me home alone. At first she would cry and pace around a bit, but I assured her that they would come back, and sure enough they always did.

Eventually, Speck started to chill out a bit and I caught her giving me that look. You know the one I mean ladies! That, 'I do like you, and do want to get to know you, but I am still quite scared of you' look.

I decided to play it cool and hard to get. I know you ladies find that simply irresistible. It was very hard, as I had to resist the urge to flop my front end down, leave my back end up and go into full 'play bow' mode. I even managed to keep my tail under control, well, sort of.

All my hard work, restraint and perseverance paid off, as one day when Mum and Dad returned from a short outing away at the shops without us, the back door was opened, and to my utter joy, Speck charged out like a rocket and actually wanted to play my favourite game of 'chase me, chase me!' I was so excited at finally being invited to play, that I went into full on charge mode and must have scared the hell out of her, because she suddenly turned round and did this sort of multiple jaw snapping thing which scared me to death! She looked just like that terrifying creature I saw in this film I sat and watched with Mum and Dad on the TV box. It was about an Alien. I would most definitely remember to be more respectful during my games with Speck in future.

Everything was going so well and we were all bonding wonderfully as a pack, when disaster struck……………..

Chapter 36

SPECK'S HEALTH SCARE

It was about a week after Speck had come to live with us, and Mum and Speck were playing in the garden. I had already had my run and play with Moo, my cow toy because Speck preferred me not to be there when she had her run and play with her favourite toy Jaffy the giraffe. She likes to play with Mum and I like to play with Speck and the two don't mix. We always have our special run and play time separately – even to this day.

Speck was charging around the garden having a great time, when suddenly she stopped and started to cough violently. She dropped Jaffy, and even from my vantage point indoors on the sofa, I could see that something was very wrong.

Mum rushed over to her, and Speck sort of sagged and tried to walk, but her legs were shaking too much. Mum supported her and was rubbing her chest and talking to her, but Speck looked terrified. She couldn't breathe and was so scared that she was making this awful, pitiful whining noise. Mum managed to get her indoors and I rushed over to see if she was ok. Mum asked me to sit on my bed, which I did, but I so wanted to go over and see what was wrong with my girl. Mum got Speck onto the sofa-bed and ran to get the phone. Poor Speck wanted to lie down, but every time she tried to, she had to keep sitting back up and holding her head up so that her nose was in the air to try to get some air down to her lungs. She was still making that pitiful whining noise and her eyes were filled with terror. Mum sat next to her and stroked her chest, whilst making a call to our vet. Luckily, the surgery is just down the end of our road, and usually we walk there, but Speck was in no fit state to walk, she would have to go in the car.

By the time Mum had finished talking on the phone, Speck had started to look a bit better. Her breathing, though still very heavy and fast, was slowly returning to normal and she was relaxing a little bit. Mum waited another few minutes, and when Speck was able to walk, she slowly walked her out to the car. I wanted to go as well, because I wanted to make sure Speck was ok, and also didn't want to miss the opportunity of making a fuss of my good pal John, the vet.

I know that many of my kind are vet-haters, but I absolutely adore my vet. I love everyone actually, but I especially love my vet, John. We have this sort of understanding you see. I have had to endure some very personal and embarrassing procedures in his consulting room, but I am always rewarded for my good natured tolerance with treats! So, I make his job a lot easier by being a model patient and he makes my trips to his surgery much more pleasant by feeding me treats and making a huge fuss of me. I like to think that I am one of his favourite clients, but he is a very nice man and is probably just as nice to all of his regulars.

Despite my efforts to get into the car, Mum made me stay at home. I was a bit upset and felt very left out, but I realised that Speck was in trouble and it would be a lot easier for everyone if I stayed out of the way and waited at home. After all, I would want to make a fuss of John, and he would obviously want to make a fuss of me, but Speck needed his help that day, so I would just have to have double treats and fuss next time I saw him.

Anyway, back to our poor Speck....

By the time they got to see John, Speck was almost back to her old self again. Mum explained exactly what had happened and Speck was given a thorough check over. John said that he wasn't sure, but she may have a problem with her heart and he wanted to refer her to a specialist vet called a cardiologist for tests.

It meant that Speck would have to go into hospital for a whole day, but if it meant that she would never have another one of those horrid attacks again where she couldn't breathe, then it would be worth it. So it was arranged and we waited for the appointment to come through.

Mum informed Jodie at the kennels and she was shocked and very upset. Speck was only 2 and her life was only just beginning. It would be very cruel if it did turn out to be a serious heart problem, as this would mean that Speck would never be able to run fast off leash in case she literally dropped dead.

At the kennels, hounds are just gently walked and Speck had been checked by the vet before her pre-happiness operation and nothing was found then. This problem had only come to light because she had been running hard and fast in our garden.

Speck had been living with us 24/7 for a week and we didn't know that she had a problem either. Jodie offered to help in any way she could. She had rescued Speck and cared for her for many months and was as shocked and upset as we all were. Mum promised to keep Jodie informed at all times.

The appointment duly came through, and we all went to the hospital with Speck to see the special heart vet man. We stayed with her as long as we were allowed to, but eventually we had to leave her there. It was very sad, as she thought we didn't want her any more. Mum and Dad promised we would collect her later. They gave her a cuddle and wished her luck. I gave her a little kiss on her nose and told her to be brave. I assured her that we were coming back for her later but I don't think she believed us. She looked back at us as they led her away and she looked so sad. We all felt miserable. As the hospital was a long way from home, we spent the day in a nearby park, and Mum had packed food for us all.

Speck had only been with us for a week, but it felt strange her not being there. I hoped she would be ok. I had only just found her and we were just becoming best pals. She was such a young girl with her whole life ahead of her. I couldn't lose her now.

We had as good a day as we could in the park, when

at last, it was time to go and collect Speck from the hospital. Mum had called and they said that she was ok, but still sleepy from the anaesthetic (I remember that feeling, it's very nice actually). We went back to the hospital and waited to speak to the heart man.

Eventually we were called through to see him and there was a lot of talk going on. It seemed that Speck did have a very slight heart murmur, and a tiny leak in one of her valves, but he said that this was very common and quite normal in Greyhounds, as they have such big hearts – in more ways than one. Their hearts are physically bigger in size than other dog's, to enable more blood and oxygen to be pumped through to help them to cope with the speed at which they run. And of course they are big because they are so full of love to give to everyone!

He said that these minor defects would not affect her in any way, and even better still, would not affect her life expectancy. So that meant that Speck would be able to run and play with me forever! I was so relieved I can tell you, as were Mum and Dad.

The heart man said that it was fluid in Speck's lungs that was the cause of her collapse in the garden and her being unable to breathe. Our vet had detected the minor heart problems, but had also mentioned that she had some congestion in her lungs. The heart man said that the fluid could possibly have been the residue from an old lungworm infestation that she had picked up in Ireland, before she was rescued and taken to the kennels. Of course all the hounds are wormed at the kennels, but she almost certainly would have had these parasites when she was in Ireland, which could explain why she did so badly in her races over there.

We were told that it would take some time for her lungs to clear completely, and that there was a slight possibility of some permanent scarring, but all in all it was really very good news. Speck was to have some special magic powder in her dinner to help to decongest her lungs.

As the heart man was explaining things to Mum and Dad, I could hear a little whimpering in the back room and recognised it as Speck's voice. I was straining on the leash to get round there to see her and I started to woof to her. She woofed back and as the heart man was having trouble speaking over our woofing, he went to get her.

Speck came wobbling around the corner and we all smothered her with hugs and kisses. Even her tail was wagging. Something she hadn't done before. She was obviously pleased that we had come back for her. She was very tired still, so once the initial greetings were done, she flopped down on the floor and went to sleep while the heart man carried on chatting to Mum and Dad. I laid on the floor next to Speck and watched her sleeping. She was such a beautiful girl and I was so proud that she was MY girl, and would be forever.

Once all the medical banter was done and the humungous bill was paid (Speck is worth it), Dad lifted Speck into the car and we all went off home. Speck slept all the way home. She went out for a wee, albeit very wobbly, then she went straight back to sleep and only woke up again for dinner later. She had slept for most of the day and all of the previous night too. Wonderful things those sleep injections!

Mum called Jodie and told her the good news. Jodie was as relieved as us and asked Mum to give Speck a great big hug and a kiss from her and all of her old friends at the kennels.

Mum wouldn't let Speck run in the garden for a long while after that, but we went for brisker walks than usual to help her to clear her lungs. As the heart man had predicted, Speck was coughing like an old man on 60 a day for a while. It was the medicine that she was taking, doing its stuff and clearing all the muck out of her lungs and throat. I must say, her breath is not good in the mornings at the best of times, but during those days on the medicine, she could have peeled the paint off of the walls with that breath! I tried to be polite, but even I, who am partial to raiding smelly old food bins, could not muster the stamina to give her a good morning kiss!

Thankfully, Speck made a full recovery and is now as disgustingly healthy as me. She still has terrible bog breath in the mornings though!

Chapter 37

SPECK MEETS THE KENT PACK

Once Speck had recovered from her hospital ordeal, we all went down to Kent to proudly introduce our new pack member to the rest of the family.

Of course, she was very shy and reserved, but well-mannered and polite. Everyone said how sweet she was, and totally the opposite to me. I wasn't sure quite how to take that, but decided it was sort of a compliment, meaning that I am very outgoing and not nervous around strangers. I hope that's what they meant anyway.

We had a nice day, meeting up with everyone and as I had told her she would do, Speck received a lot of fuss from the whole family. I did too as usual. I think she was a little overwhelmed by the size of our extended pack, but she handled it very well, and everyone was very careful how they approached her. Mum and Dad had warned them all of her screaming fits if she got scared, so they were all extra gentle with her.

The little people were their usual rowdy selves though, and chased her around the table a few times, just trying to stroke her of course, but she was terrified of them and just wanted to escape.

I of course love them, and invited them to chase me instead, which they happily did. Mum had to protect Speck from them to stop her getting too stressed out. Nowadays she mucks in and is quite au fait with them all, but in the early days, the poor girl was absolutely terrified of them.

It was not a party day, just a nice, quiet visit to introduce Speck to the pack and all too soon it was time to go home, so we said our goodbyes and off we went.

Speck seemed relieved to be in the car. Unlike me, she never got car sick and was a good traveller, so again, unlike me, she often saw the car as a place of sanctuary. To me, it was always a nightmare on wheels, a place to be dreaded and feared.

The day had all been a bit overwhelming for her, but she did enjoy meeting everyone and getting loads of attention.

We had also had a good run in Aunty Carol and Uncle Rob's big garden and we both slept all the way home. It was a good day.

Chapter 38

THE ROUTINES OF EVERYDAY PACK LIFE

Mum and Dad went back to work, and me and Speck had the house to ourselves for most of the day. It was a nice, quiet time when we could have some time alone together to just enjoy being friends and get to know each other better.

We would sleep most of the day away on our 'forever sofa', and when we were awake, we would choose a toy to play with.

Mum knew that we would not argue over things, so she would leave the entire contents of our toy box scattered on the floor. Of course whichever toy Speck chose, I decided I would like to play with and vice versa. Rather than fight and argue, in the early days, we had a very civilised toy swapping routine.......

If I wanted Speck's toy, I would choose another one and pretend that I really was enjoying playing with it. She would get very interested, thinking my toy was much more fun than hers, so then she would leave her toy and pretend to choose a different one. I would immediately dash over and grab the one that she originally had, and she would go and pinch the one that I originally had. This was fine for a few minutes, then I would begin to wonder if the toy that I first had was maybe more fun than the one that Speck first had. I think she might have been thinking the same, because when I pretended to choose another toy, she would grab the one that I had pinched from her.

Confused? Tell me about it! This procedure could go on for hours and kept us out of mischief until the rest of the pack got home.

It would have been nice to have a game of 'tugga' with Speck, but we were both much too respectful of each other to do this, and would just politely let each other take the rope toy instead of hanging on to it for grim death, tugging and growling like mad things.

Nowadays if I want her toy, I either use the civilised toy swapping routine as just explained, or make out I had found a pot of gold (a piece of cheese under the sofa). This never fails to get her attention and she always leaves her toy and comes running over.

Nowadays if she wants my toy, she just comes over and takes it. I know my place and let her have it, no questions asked. I vividly remember those Alien Jaws snapping at me at lightning speed and have no wish to ever see them again!

As much as I like to think that I wear the 'pack leader trousers', I am loathe to admit that I share joint 2nd place with Dad. The girls are equally in charge, which Dad tells me is normal pack hierarchy wherever or whoever you are in the world.

During the next few months, Speck really made herself at home, and started to come out of her little shell. She even started to wag her tail when Mum and Dad came home, at meal times and walkies times. She was finally starting to put her past behind her and enjoy her new life with us. It was lovely to see.

I taught her lots of really neat tricks in those first few months. The best one was, if she fidgeted in the night and got cold and wanted to be tucked back in, there were 3 ways to wake Mum and Dad up……

1/ Stand next to their bed and shake, so that your ears slapped on your neck and made a really loud noise. If that failed………..

2/ Locate an ear or eyelid under the duvet and stick your cold nose on it, whilst making squeaky noises. If that also failed…………

3/ Launch yourself high into the air and land square on top of them, and jump up and down squeaking.

Option 3 never ever failed - especially if we both did it at the same time!

Of course these days, we have polar fleece p. j's that we wear on cold nights in the winter. Mum bought them on the internet from a lovely lady in Australia and they are sooo warm and sooo comfy, that we actually ask to have them put on before going to bed on chilly nights. All of us short-coated Sighthounds feel the cold and should have some. They are great!

Dad went bonkers when Mum told him she was ordering them and he had a real hissy fit about me wearing pj's. He said that he would refuse to let me in the garden in the mornings if I still had them on, but Mum argued that it was mainly her that got woken up several times in the night to cover us back up with our duvets. She said that she was fed up with not getting one single, decent night's sleep all of the previous winter; what with him snoring and me needing to be covered up, and now that there were two hounds to take it in turns to wake her up, we were having fleece pyjamas and that was that!

To be honest, Dad often got woken up too, but always pretended to be fast asleep so that Mum would have to get out of bed to see to us.

So our jammies duly arrived all the way from the land down under. Mine are macho blue camo print, and Speck's are girly pink, with a paw print motif on one back leg. They keep us toasty all night, and now Mum manages to stay awake at work all day. Even Dad has to admit that they are a godsend. He still won't let me in the garden wearing them though.

A few other very useful things that I taught Speck :-

1/ Where all the local cats live and where they sit at which times of day.

2/ Which is 'bin night' and whose bins usually smell nicest.

3/ How to detect signs that a bath is imminent (water running upstairs and Mum and Dad looking very shifty) and how to plan your escape.

4/ If you fail to escape in time and are unfortunately captured and subjected to the horrendous bathing procedure that humans feel is necessary in order for us to share their home, where the best places to dry yourself are (on, or preferably in their bed and especially on their pillows!).

5/ How to detect signs that visitors are coming (house is extra tidy and our paws are wiped before we come in).

6/ How to detect signs that we are going visiting (our toys, bowls and a bag of food are put in a bag).

Walkies and mealtimes are so obvious that Speck needed no help with those ones.

There are also some great tricks that Mum and Dad have taught us both, including: sit, wait, 'gimme 5' (give paw), and catch the flying treat. We are both very clever hounds.

It soon seemed like Speck had been living with us all her life, and as the weeks went by, she gradually emerged completely from her protective shell and morphed into the beautiful, happy, confident and sometimes very bossy lady that she is today. Rather like a beautiful butterfly escaping from its ugly old chrysalis. As I said before, I do watch lots of nature programs on the TV box!

We have a happy, relaxed life. Mum and Dad go out to work to earn money to keep us in the lifestyle we have grown accustomed to, and we have lovely days relaxing on our sofa, sleeping and playing. We are never left longer than 4 or 5 hours and Mum always comes home at lunchtimes to give us our dinner and let us in the garden for wees. We get a fuss and a play and she has a few minutes spare to get her lunch, then off she goes back to work again and we go back for a nice sleep on our sofa until she gets home again.

Life wasn't good for either of us to begin with, but we have landed on our paws now and enjoy a very nice life, thank you very much! We deserve it though, as do all dogs.

Chapter 39

OPEN DAY AT THE VETS

There was an open day at our vets one Sunday in November, so Mum and Dad walked us down to see what it was all about.

The place was heaving with people and dogs, and there were stalls and things inside the surgery and competitions taking place in the car park.

I used to be very friendly to ALL dogs, no matter what size, shape, colour, breed or gender they were, but for some reason, since my Speck came to live with me, I sometimes get this ugly jealous streak rise up from somewhere deep inside me if another dog pays her too much attention.

It's ok if it's another girl of course, but if a male gets a bit too friendly, I can't help myself. I warn them off with a loud grumbly growl and all my fur comes up along my back, which is quite uncomfortable I can tell you.

Now, I am not a vicious dog at all and it's all noise and hot air with me, but sometimes, other dog's humans think that I am this ferocious, rabid beast that should be feared and avoided at all costs. This is not the case, but this is sometimes the message that I unintentionally convey to the human on the other end of the nuisance dog's lead.

Of course, this is exactly what I want the offending dog to think, but they usually take one look at me, realise it's all a big bluff, and say, "yeah, right!".

Their human on the other hand, is terrified and drags their dog away. So it sort of works in a round-a-bout way, but I really don't intend to frighten people. I love people and would never ever hurt them. It's just that I feel this need to protect my girl from all other male dogs that might want to try and take her away from me. Because of this, I am sometimes misunderstood by some people who are not true 'doggie people', and don't fully understand my actions and the reason behind them. There was one such person at the vets that day................

I had already warned off two over-boisterous Weimaraner pups that were lunging towards me in a clumsy attempt at asking me to play. I can get a bit grumpy with over-boisterous pups with no manners, even though I was one myself not so long ago.
 Suddenly the door opened, and in the doorway stood a very tough, aggressive looking crossbreed. Our eyes locked and we both took an instant dislike to each other. He made the first move and lunged towards me, snarling and snapping. Of course, I couldn't be seen to look cowardly in front of my lady, so I retaliated with a barrage of aggressive barks. It was chaos and the offending dog was taken outside. Mum dragged me over to another room and peace was resumed once more. I said hello to all the other dogs and their humans and we mingled for a while. Occasionally, me and the aggressive crossbreed crossed paths again, and we would both go into a

barking frenzy as soon as we clapped eyes on each other, and there was no way we would get along. I was scared stiff of him to be honest, and was just putting on a front, but wasn't about to let him know that.

His humans just glared at Mum and Dad and made no attempt to make the usual embarrassed banter that normal, experienced doggie people make when their dogs embarrass them. Mum did try to speak to them, but they muttered something abusive and dragged their snarling mutt away.

There were a few competitions going on in the car park, and Mum looked down the list to see if we could be entered for any. Unfortunately there were no classes suitable for Speck. Had there been a most beautiful girl class, she would have nailed that paws down, but sadly there was nothing that she could be entered for; however, there was one class that I was perfect for……..'The waggiest tail' class! I was duly entered and eagerly went to line up.

The winner was to be decided by the amount of applause that they received from the crowd (it was only a fun thing after all) and there were a lot of us lined up wagging furiously to warm up.

The competition was hot, and when it came to my turn, I was proud to actually be able to put my raw, natural talent to good use. After years of trying to conceal my talent, all that pent up energy was released and the old back end went wild. I produced the biggest, windmilliest butt I have ever had, and I ended my display with an awe inspiring snake.

The crowd loved it and I was getting thunderous applause for my gargantuan efforts, when all of a sudden there was all this boo-ing and hissing and shouting at the back.

I stopped in mid wriggle and looked round in confusion to see who could possible find my efforts so worthy of all this negative response.

There to my right, was the snarling, growling crossbreed with his snarling, growling human pack, all shouting abuse at me.

The rest of the crowd were horrified, and Mum turned a delicate shade of crimson. Even the judge said in a very loud voice that no booing was called for.

Nobody could quite believe that people could be so petty and do something like that. It was, after all, supposed to be just a fun event. It was terrible. I had been ridiculed in front of everyone, but as Mum and everyone who spoke to us told me, they were just making themselves look incredibly stupid and childish.

The ironic thing was that Mum had applauded the nasty mutt earlier, when he was standing there looking totally ridiculous, wearing a human's saggy old T-shirt, in an attempt at winning the best dressed dog class. But then my Mum and Dad are not petty humans and would never take revenge on any animal, and would certainly never launch a public attack to try and ruin its chances in a competition.

Despite all the commotion, I was awarded second place in the waggiest tail competition, and although the winner was a worthy winner, I still can't help wondering if I might have won first place if it hadn't been for that nasty crossbreed and his even nastier human pack. Anyway, second place was a very honourable achievement and not to be sniffed at. My certificate is proudly displayed on the side of the fridge freezer.

The side of the fridge freezer is mine and Speck's special place, where doggy certificates and poems are displayed so that me and Speck can look at them while we are laying on our 'forever sofa' together. There's a lovely photo of me and Speck which was taken on the first day that we ever met.

What a very lucky day that was for me!

Chapter 40

LAMINATED NIGHTMARES

As I believe I have already mentioned, I have a few little phobias……..

My biggest and scariest phobia is shiny, slippery floor surfaces.

I was so relieved when I first set paw into my new home, to find that the floors were made of this great natural wood, that you could just sink your claws into to get a brilliant grip. It was marvellous stuff. While Mum and Dad were out at work, me and Speck would spend many happy afternoons tearing around the house at top speed, digging our claws into the lovely wooden floor and never slipping over.

We would frequently use the house as a race track and in doing so, made the lovely wood even more practical for our claws as it was getting rougher and rougher on the surface. You could even see an actual 'track' that we had gouged out and we were very pleased with it indeed.

Mum and Dad it seems were not!

One day, as me and Speck were sprawled on our sofa, relaxing after a particularly enjoyable race around the house circuit, Mum and Dad said "we are just popping out".

We both slid off the sofa yawning and mustering the energy for a walkies, when we were told that we were staying home and they were going out alone.

We were a bit miffed but soon forgave them and

clambered back up on the sofa to resume our chilling session. It was no big deal. We were tired out after our race anyway.

Mum and Dad were gone for about an hour and when they returned, Dad kept going back out to the car to bring these long, heavy looking packets indoors. He carefully stacked them in the front room under the table, and they both looked extremely pleased with themselves.

Humans are complex creatures and I sometimes don't even try to figure out what they are up to. Me and Speck went to investigate these strange packages, but after a thorough sniffing, we deduced that they were not food or toys for us, so we went back to the sofa to continue with our snoozing.

The packets sat under the table for several days, until one day, Dad stayed at home.

Me and Speck watched with interest as Dad took the packets out from under the table one at a time and laid the contents, which were boards of some sort, onto our racetrack.

I wasn't too bothered to begin with, but as our beloved track slowly began to disappear underneath these boards, I began to get very worried indeed. This was looking very serious, so I decided to go and check this out. It was very strange.

Dad was putting new, thinner wood strips on top of the old ones. WHY?! I again reminded myself that humans are strange creatures and sometimes do things that make absolutely no sense whatsoever.

Obviously, this was one of those times. It meant that

me and Speck would have to start from scratch, gouging out a new track. What a waste of time and energy! As I said, it made no sense whatsoever.

I decided to check this new track material out, so I put a paw on it and almost died of shock. This looked like our lovely wood track, but it was not. It was actually a very hard, shiny and slippery imposter!

I ran back to the safety of our sofa and conveyed an urgent telepathic message to Speck, informing her of this terrible disaster.

She was obviously a little miffed, but just said 'oh well, we will get used to it I suppose'. Speck has phobias of her own, but shiny floors are not one of them. I realised that Dad was quite possibly going to put this terrifying stuff all over the entire floor and panic started to set in.

After a while, Dad stopped and I could breathe again. Thank God for that, at least I would still have some proper floor to stand on without breaking my neck. But to my great disappointment, the next day, it started all over again. I was slowly being hemmed in on the sofa, and had to resort to tiptoeing around a small gap around the edges of the floor, which with my giraffe limbs and big feet, was no mean feat to be sniffed at I can tell you. I must have looked like a furry ballet dancer that needed a wee real bad. Speck was not very sympathetic and soon got the hang of walking and even running on this evil new floor, but once the few inches of my beloved wood floor around the edges had disappeared, I then had to leap onto the sofa from the safety of the rug. The rug would slide from under my paws as I took off, due to the fact that it was sitting on top of that evil slippery floor, and I would end up in a crumpled heap a few inches from the safety of the sofa. I would then have to try to stand up and re-launch myself off of this ice rink like surface.

Mum and Dad kept saying "Oh poor Sonic" and made sympathetic noises, but if they really were sorry, why the hell didn't they rip this evil slippery stuff up and let me have my lovely, comforting, scruffy, gouged up wooden floorboards back?!

I went to bed a nervous wreck that night, and drifted into a very uneasy, restless sleep. I thought that I was safe up in the bedroom on the carpet and my duvet. Safe from the evil floor, but it came and attacked me during the night while I slept! Really, it did! These slippery, hard boards were flying out of the packets and chasing me around the room, slapping down hard on the floor with a loud bang right behind me. As fast as I ran to try and escape, I couldn't shake them off. They were just inches away from my twizzle. I ran round and round until eventually I was cornered over by the fridge freezer. As I cowered in fear, I looked up just in time to see the last plank coming down on my head, then it went black and the next thing I knew was that I was screaming the house down, and Mum and Dad had leapt out from under their duvet and had come rushing over to see who was murdering me in my bed!

I was shaking and terrified, and it took me ages and lots of reassuring cuddles before I was calm enough to get back to sleep.

Speck looked over, decided that I was just being a silly wuss again and promptly went back to sleep. Nice!

I kept telling myself that it was just a silly nightmare and it wasn't true. Eventually, I drifted back off to sleep, when suddenly, I remembered that it wasn't just a nightmare, it was actually true and those killer planks were actually downstairs! AAAAGGGHHH!!!

The 2 lessons that I learnt from all this, is that:-

1/ sometimes humans do have a reason for doing silly things that initially make no sense. Our racetrack, lovely as it was, would eventually have worn out and we would have got serious splinters in our pads, and would have had to have gone to the vet for painful treatments.

2/ As I had previously learnt on my first day at home, In order to conquer your fears and phobias, you really do have to face them.

I am happy to report that I am now able to walk on laminate flooring with just a mild twinge of fear, which hopefully will go completely in time.

I thought that Mum and Dad were being really cruel by putting those evil planks down over our track, but I later realised that they were actually thinking of me. So, I forgave them………….eventually………

Chapter 41

SPECK MEETS THE MAGICAL TREE

It was getting near one my favourite times of the year. It was almost Christmas again! It was the time for goodwill to all dogs, and treats and toys galore! I had told Speck what happens at Christmas, but she didn't quite understand just how exciting it would be.

The day finally came when Dad went into the ceiling and came down with the long box, containing the plastic tree that I had been so tempted to wee up the year before. I warned Speck to keep her nose out of the way as he came down the metal stairs. I remembered that painful snout from last year too!

I could hardly contain my excitement as I sat and watched Speck sniffing the box. I knew what was in there and I hoped that she would be as awestruck as I had been when it was made into a tree and all the glittery bits and lights were put on it.

The birds were getting excited too. They had seen this ritual for several years now and even they got excited at Christmas time. They like the magical tree and know that when it appears, presents follow soon after.

Speck had no idea what Christmas was. I did though, and I knew that she was in for a real treat.

Mum came home carrying lots of bags of shopping. Me and Speck always like to check out the bags, and were disappointed to find that there were no tasty smelling food items in any of them. We did, however, detect a faint whiff of our favourite shop. Mum had sneakily been to the pet shop and not taken us. I was disgusted with her. How could she! She knew it was our favourite place in the whole world, apart from the nice charity shop down the road where we are always welcomed and fussed, oh, and our own home of course.

Then I realised that the reason we had not been invited, was because she had been secretly getting our prezzies to give to the big, fat Santa man in the red suit to bring for us the night before Christmas. This theory was confirmed when she told me to go away and stop being so nosey.

She picked up one of the bags and rummaged around inside, then pulled something out shouting "ta da!" We all looked over and saw that she was holding two red things with big white fluffy balls on the ends. Dad started to make noises of protest, but knew from experience that it was wasted breath, so carried on getting the tree out whilst muttering to himself.

Mum came over to me and Speck and plonked the red things on our heads, then rushed off to get her camera. They were apparently called Santa hats, and some dogs wear them at Christmas. The year before, I had antlers. What on earth would we be forced to wear next year?

We don't mind wearing things really. It's quite fun because it makes Mum and the little people smile. Dad, however, is never impressed when we wear clothes or hats, and always mutters under his breath disapprovingly.

Aunty Debs had bought us some really nice 'snow pup' T-shirts to wear for Christmas day, and Mum also had red bow ties in the bag, so we were going to be very festive hounds indeed. Dad was not going to be impressed with our costumes this year!

Mum scurried up the wooden hill with her bags of 'secret' shopping and obviously we tried to follow her, but were told to go back down and stay with Dad and the bedroom door was firmly shut.

We strained our ears and noses outside the door for any clues as to the contents of the bags and amongst much rustling of paper and peeling of sellotape noises, we suddenly heard a faint but very distinctive squeak. Yahooo! We were definitely getting squeaky toys on the big day!

I love squeaky toys, but Speck is obsessed with them and could not contain her excitement. She let out a little squeal and promptly blew our cover. We were rumbled. Mum threw open the door and ordered us to go away immediately. She followed us down and shut the door just to make sure that we didn't sneak back up to listen outside the bedroom door. Mum can be a real spoilsport at times!

Dad was getting on well with the tree assembly and I knew that the sparkly bits and lights would soon be going on, so we decided to stay and watch.

I was getting quite excited waiting to see what Speck would think of the finished tree. I knew that it was a truly magical tree, and I hoped that she would love it as much as I do.

We both lay quietly on the sofa side by side; watching as Dad carefully wound the sparkly rope around the branches and hung the little balls on the ends. Of course I remembered this ritual from last year, but Speck was looking very puzzled. She looked at me for an explanation for Dad's bizarre behaviour, but I just told her to be patient and watch, wait and be amazed. She still looked baffled, but also had a wide-eyed excited look on her face. She snuggled a bit closer to me and resumed her observation with even more intensity.

Finally Dad shouted "finished!" and stepped back for a final appraisal of his creation. A few seconds later, Mum emerged from upstairs and we all looked at the tree together. Dad bent down and flicked the switch and the magical tree came alive, just like last year.

I looked at Speck and her eyes were like saucers! She went to move closer for a better look, but the lights twinkled and she backed off again. She sat up staring into the branches, totally mesmerised, just like I was the year before. I just knew she would love it and I was so happy to have been right.

By nature, we hounds spend a lot of time just looking around, and take notice of anything new in our surroundings. We are not called Sighthounds for nothing. We really do study things quite intensely, especially if it's something that we like the look of, or if we are trying to figure out what it actually is. In this instance, it was both!

Speck eventually settled down next to me and we both lay stretched out with our chins resting on our knees, gazing at the glowing, magical tree.

After a while, I glanced at Speck and she had fallen asleep. She looked very content, and as my eyelids grew heavier, I thought what a truly wonderful, special time of year Christmas was.

Chapter 42

OUR FIRST CHRISTMAS TOGETHER

For the next few days, me and Speck had lots of fun stealing the shiny balls off of the magical tree and playing fetch with them, like I did last year. We got told off of course, but they were such good fun that we just couldn't help ourselves.

It was really nice, because Mum and Dad were both at home with us most of the time. It was very cold outside and we had to have our fleece coats on and be coaxed for ages before we could be persuaded to go for a walk. It was so lovely and cosy once we got back home though, that it was worth going out in the cold, just to have that lovely warm feeling of coming back home again.

Well, the big day eventually arrived and there was much excitement in our house that the morning. As soon as Mum and Dad woke up, they said happy Christmas to each other, then invited us both up onto the bed for a special Christmas cuddle. It was lovely. Dad went down to make tea and breakfast, and we followed him down for ours and to do our first biz of the day, but most importantly, to check under the tree!

The birds were extra chirpy and had obviously realised that it was the big day, and that they would soon be getting their presents.

We would be going to Aunty Carol and Uncle Rob's house for the day with Mum and Dad, and all the pack would be there, but the birds would be staying at home. Mum said to Dad that she felt bad leaving them home alone on Christmas day, but they get a bit stressed in the car and it was very cold outside too. They are happy to stay home together and there would no doubt be new toys and something nice to nibble on in their Christmas stockings.

Dad wished the bird's happy Christmas and put their TV box on for them, and then went back up the wooden hill with the breakfast tray leaving them happily chirping away to Christmas songs. We had already scoffed our breakfast and been out to the loo, so went back up to bed for a while too. I was getting very excited, wondering what squeaky I would get and what delicious treats awaited me in my stocking.

I remembered my very first Christmas present last year. It was my squeaky blue dog with the rope legs. I still had him and hoped that I always would. I love all my toys and would hate to lose any of them. Luckily, Mum is very good and sews them up for me when they get a bit worse for wear and so far, I have managed to keep them all. Of course they have all been munched on and thrown around the house and garden, so none of them squeak any more. Because of this, I really get excited at the thought of a brand new toy that actually squeaks!

As I mentioned earlier, Speck is even more squeaky obsessed than me, so it would soon be very noisy in our house. Eventually Mum and Dad had finished their tea and breakfast and were getting out of bed. Yippee, it was prezzie time at last!

We all went down the hill and Mum said, "Right then, shall we see who has been good girls and boys this year, and have been left a prezzie from Santa?" I love everyone, but I especially love this Santa guy. He's just so nice, going out in the cold, delivering presents for us and he doesn't even really know us. I wondered why he did it, especially as Mum had already had them at home once for wrapping up when she came home from the pet shop. It really didn't make much sense, but then as I always say, humans often don't.

It was a really nice of him to do it though and I suppose it gave him a job.

I was so excited by this time that I really needed another wee, but it was very cold out there, so I just tried not to think about it.

I was disappointed that Mum decided to hand out presents for the birds first, but she said that they wouldn't be coming with us, so should have preferential treatment while we were at home. I suppose she had a valid point, but the suspense was killing me!

Dad was excited too and was pestering for a present, but he got told by Mum to wait his turn like the rest of us. Speck was getting really excited, but wasn't sure why, or what was going on. I had tried to explain it all, but she would find out soon enough, just how exciting getting prezzies was.

The little birds with the tufty hats don't open their presents, so Mum did it for them and they were soon happily playing with new toys and sampling various seed things that were dangling in their little houses.

We had to wait while Jack parrot opened his presents himself. It took him ages and I wondered if he was stalling on purpose just so we had to wait longer for ours. I wouldn't put it past the sneaky, manipulative featherbag, but hey, it was the time of peace and goodwill to all men, dogs and even birds, so I decided to let it go…just this once.

Finally, it was our turn and we both sat quivering with anticipation as Mum delved into our Christmas stockings. There was a squeak from Speck's one as Mum rummaged and we both jumped up and rushed over. Mum made us sit back down again and she pulled out a similar shaped parcel from each stocking and held them up.

I really wished that I had asked to go out for a wee, as I almost disgraced myself at that point. We both started to whine with excitement, and Mum held out the parcels for us. I grabbed mine and rushed over to the sofa to rip the paper off. Speck took hers, but was a bit confused as to what to do with it.

As I pinned my parcel down, it made a loud squeak and Speck immediately dropped her parcel and came rushing over. I gave her that 'no way Hosé' look and she backed off. Christmas or not, this squeaky was mine! Mum called her over and gave her the present again. She took it up onto the sofa and dropped it.

Mum went over and gave it a squeeze. As it made a loud squeaking noise, Speck got the message and pounced on it and started ripping the paper off. Like a thing possessed she was! Speck had unwrapped her very first Christmas present, and like me, needed no further coaxing to open the others.

Mum and Dad opened a present from each other, but they were very boring presents. No rawhide chews or squeaky toys in their parcels. Ours on the other paw, were to die for!

After a couple of hours, it was time to drive down to Kent to meet up with the rest of the pack. I told Speck that there might be more parcels at Aunty Carol and Uncle Rob's for us and she was in the car like a shot! This girl was getting the hang of Christmas very quickly!

On arrival at Aunty Carol and Uncle Rob's house, we were ritually dressed in our Christmas outfits in the driveway. This was not good, as it was very cold, and very public. But it was worth suffering the hypothermia and sniggers from passers-by just to see the big smiles on the little people's faces as we trotted in wearing our Christmas T-shirts, Santa hats and bow ties.

We had a lovely day and as I suspected, there were lots more presents from the rest of the pack and a very special Christmas dinner of beef and turkey.

It got very noisy, what with our new squeakers, the little people playing with their noisy new toys and the big people chatting and laughing, but it was great.

Speck wasn't nervous any more, even with all that racket going on, and a great Christmas day was had by all.

At the end of the day, we said our goodbyes, climbed into the car and headed off home. It was really cold, but we soon got all warm and snuggly and were so tired that we slept all the way home.

The birds were pleased to see us, and had also had a good day judging by the bare plastic strips dangling from their roofs. Those strips had been coated with seed when we left that morning. They all looked very fat!

We had more presents to unwrap and eat and play with, and Mum and Dad opened all of theirs too, then we all snuggled up together on the big sofa to watch the TV box for the rest of the evening.

We were all laying there in a warm, cosy, tangled heap of arms, legs, paws, cushions and tails. As I watched the magical tree lights twinkling in the low lit room, I thought to myself that Christmas certainly was a very special time, and was even more special this year now that I had my Speck to share it with.

Chapter 43

MY NEW YEAR WISHES

It was New Year's Eve just before midnight, when Mum told us to make a wish when the big clock on the TV box bonged for the twelfth time. She said she would tell us when it was time. Mum is very nice, but she sometimes underestimates how intelligent I am. I can actually count up to over 20, so didn't need to be told when the clock bonged for the twelfth time. But I didn't take offence as it was sweet of her to offer I suppose.

Dad topped up their drinks (he had already had a couple, so didn't notice that I had sneaked some from his glass) and we all sat together waiting for the big count down.

As the countdown began, I looked around my home.

I saw the magical tree twinkling and shining like a beautiful beacon of peace and happiness. I saw my many beloved toys scattered around the floor. I looked through the kitchen into the front room and saw the birds sleepily nodding off on their perches surrounded by their new toys. They even had their own slightly smaller but just as Magical Christmas tree and TV box in there. We were all very spoilt really.

I looked up at Mum and Dad, my two cherished humans that had welcomed me into their pack and provided me with a safe and loving home, where I would spend the rest of my days not having to worry about a thing. Not one thing, ever again. No more being cold and going hungry. No more feeling hurt, rejected, lonely and afraid.

I had as much food, toys, security and love that I would ever need and some spare, put by for a rainy day, just in case.

Of course it wasn't all one-sided and they had got a pretty good deal with me too. They were rewarded with daily slobbers and lots of love, fun and affection from yours truly.

Then I looked at Speck and she was looking right back at me. She is such a beautiful girl and a really good friend to me. She is my soul mate and I hope that she would say that I am hers too.

We had both been through so much in our short lives, that we would both appreciate the good times that we could now enjoy together for the rest of our lives.

As the hands on the big clock closed together on the number 12 and the twelfth bong rang out, Mum and Dad shouted "Happy New Year, make a wish everyone!"

I suddenly realised that there was nothing I needed to wish for any more. All my wishes had already been granted. So I wished that every dog could have a lovely home and a pack that loved them like mine love me, but there really was nothing that I needed to wish for, for myself.

As the old year slipped into the past and the New Year was born, I suddenly thought of a wish for myself................

Please, please, please may my life always be this good for ever and ever............

And maybe a bit more control over the old psychotic tail would be nice……..

And maybe an extra biscuit or two, or three before bedtime………

And if it could please be arranged <u>NOT</u> to rain when it's walkies time I would be grateful............

And I would prefer that Jack parrot did not try to bite my nose or twizzle at every opportunity………

And ripping up and burning the evil laminate and having my beloved old indoor racetrack back would be absolutely wonderful……

And a few more trees and lamp posts along our road would be much appreciated……………..

And maybe............

Oh, anyway, mustn't be greedy I suppose, after all there's always next year!

xx

SPECIAL MESSAGES

Firstly...to all of you great dogs who are still in kennels, patiently awaiting your 'forever sofa', and that special family to choose you.

Never give up hope, your day to shine will come.

Let me assure you that most humans are really very nice, and that if you have had a bad experience with one, this is not the norm, and when you have been rescued, your life will change for the better and will soon be filled with love and fun. You will never be scared, lonely, cold or hungry ever again.

Secondly...to all of you lovely readers that haven't already adopted a great dog from your local rescue kennels......Well, why haven't you? What are you waiting for? Go on, grab your coat and get down to the nearest kennels. There will be a little lost waif with huge, soulful eyes waiting there just for you to give him or her, the chance to brighten up your life and fill it with unconditional love.

I guarantee that you won't be sorry you went. In fact, I am so sure of this, that I am willing to stake my whole month's treat ration on it. As any dog or his/her human reading this will know, the stakes couldn't possibly get any higher than this!

Oh go on, you know you want to. A house is not a home without a dog..... or 2..... or 3..... or more. If you don't know where to go, there are some rescue kennel addresses at the back of this book.

If none of them are near to you, give one of them a call. I'm sure they will be able to put you in touch with a local kennel.

These amazing people join forces and work together all over the country and even overseas, to find perfect forever homes for the hounds that they care for so well.

At least half of the profits from the sale of this book will be donated to dog rescue charities, so well done you for buying it and helping these very special people to keep up their amazing and invaluable work to help hounds that are still waiting for a chance to start a new life.

Let's hope that all of the special, deserving dogs, large and small, that are still waiting patiently in kennels, soon find their little piece of Doggie heaven just like me and Speck did.

Anyway folks, I think that's about it. I hope that you have enjoyed reading my Autobiogwoofie as much as I enjoyed getting Mum to write it for me. ☺

Take care lovely reader.

Lots of love, wags n'slobbers,

Sonic. xx

Me a poser? I don't know what you mean!

It really, really, really did hurt!!

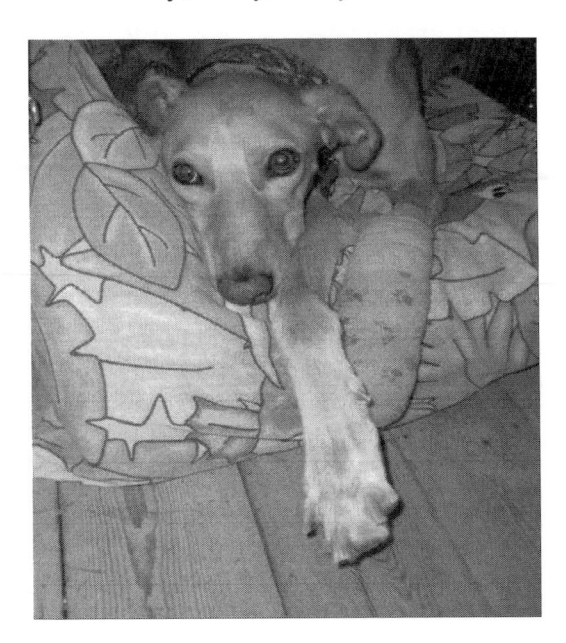

No Speck, it was definitely YOU that wee'd on him!

The stand-off between me and 'HER next door'

Writing an Autobiogwoofie is soooo exhausting!!

And so to bed…zzz….zz…zzz

The Magical Tree

Peace and goodwill to Man and Dogkind

x x x x

RESCUE CENTRES FOR GREYHOUNDS, LURCHERS AND OTHER DOGS

BATTERSEA DOGS AND CATS HOME

http://www.battersea.org.uk

Battersea, London

4 Battersea Park Road
London
SW8 4AA
Tel: 0843 509 4444

Battersea, Old Windsor

Priest Hill
Old Windsor
Windsor
Berkshire
SL4 2JN
Tel: 0843 509 4444

Battersea, Brands Hatch

Crowhurst Lane
Ash
Kent
TN15 7HH
Tel: 0843 509 4444

CASTLEDON KENNELS

http://www.castledongreyhoundrescue.co.uk

Viewing by appointment only

Castledon Kennels
181 Castledon Road
Wickford
Essex
SS12 0EG

Telephone: 01268 733293

WIMBLEDON GREYHOUND WELFARE

http://www.hershamhounds.org.uk

Wimbledon Greyhound Welfare
Burhill Kennels
Turners Lane
Hersham
Surrey
KT12 4AW

Telephone: 01932 224918

ERIN HOUNDS

http://www.erinhounds.co.uk
E-mail: email@erinhounds.co.uk

Erin Hounds
PO Box 309
Runcorn
WA7 9BQ

Telephone: Sue Coldock 01928 714558

RETIRED GREYHOUND TRUST

http://www.retiredgreyhounds.co.uk

The Greyhound Trust
Park House
Park Terrace
Worcester Park
Surrey
KT4 7JZ

Phone: 0844 826 8424
Fax: 0844 826 8425

SONIC

MY AUTOBIOGWOOFIE

Published in 2013 by
Diane Bowker

Printed in 2013 by
CPI UK

ISBN: 978-0-9574953-1-9

Revised Edition

© Copyright 2008 held by Diane Bowker

You can order further copies of this book direct via email to: sonicthelurcher@sky.com or by visiting Sonic's website: www.sonicthelurcher.com

50% of the profits from the sale of this book will be donated to dog rescue charities including Battersea Dogs and Cats home and Castledon Kennels

Thank you.